THE SPAGHETTI
SAUCE
GOURMET

160 Recipes
from Four Kinds
of Sauce

DAVID JOACHIM

FAIR WINDS
PRESS
GLOUCESTER, MASSACHUSETTS

Text © 2006 by David Joachim

First published in the USA in 2006 by
Fair Winds Press, a member of
Quayside Publishing Group
33 Commercial Street
Gloucester, MA 01930

10 09 08 07 06   1 2 3 4 5

ISBN-13: 978-1-59233-221-2
ISBN-10: 1-59233-221-8

Library of Congress Cataloging-in-Publication Data
available

Cover design by Derek Sussner
Book design by Laura McFadden
Photography by CPI

Printed and bound in China

Contents

Introduction

Spaghetti sauce is often thought of as one thing: a quick and easy way to dress up pasta. But there's so much more you can do with a jar of sauce than pour it over noodles. Think outside the pasta box. That jar of tomato sauce in your pantry could serve as the base for a braising liquid to make Braised Beef Short Ribs (page 44). It could be mixed with orange juice, saffron, and sherry to steam Mussels in Orange Saffron Sauce (page 122). Prepared pesto can form an aromatic crust on Grilled Lamb with Pesto (page 79); or it can be mixed with mashed potatoes to whip up Baked Salmon on Pesto Potato Pancakes (page 113); or slathered over a roast to make Pesto Crusted Stuffed Beef Tenderloin (page 46). Prepared Alfredo sauce has countless uses, from White Pizza with Spinach and Shrimp (page 168) to Mushroom Bisque (page 192) to Alfredo Braised Pork Shoulder (page 67).

When you think about the basic ingredients in popular pasta sauces, such as tomatoes, cream, Parmesan cheese, and basil, you begin to see the endless possibilities for using these sauces in innovative ways. Tomatoes are enjoyed in cuisines throughout the world from India to Mexico to Italy to France to Spain. Various forms of cream are used widely in the cooking of western countries. In addition to such American favorites as Easy Chicken Pot Pie (page 92), this book provides simple recipes for popular international dishes such as Shrimp Pad Thai (page 133), Yucatan-Style Shredded Pork (page 50), Moroccan Lamb with Couscous (page 80), Catalan Seafood Stew (page 199), and North Indian Chicken in Warmly Spiced Tomato Sauce (page 88).

All in all, you'll learn how to create more than 160 fabulous meals using prepared pasta sauces that are available in your supermarket.

Getting the Most from Prepared Pasta Sauces and Other Convenience Foods

How I Approached the Recipes

It was fun coming up with all of these recipes. The challenge was to use familiar ingredients in uncommon ways. Given that prepared sauces were on the menu, I figured that most readers would also be willing to take a few other shortcuts when appropriate.

The recipes here call for both fresh and prepared ingredients in an effort to make the best-tasting home-cooked meals in the least amount of time. I freely use precut produce, prepared doughs, and other good-quality convenience foods such as *real* preshredded Parmesan cheese. Using these widely available prepared foods dramatically shortens kitchen prep time. Let's face it: most of our time spent cooking actually involves chopping, slicing, dicing, or mincing onions, carrots, celery, bell peppers, garlic, or ginger. Thankfully, all of these vegetables are now available prechopped, presliced, and preminced in jars or in tubs in the refrigerated produce section of most grocery stores.

Skim through the recipes in this book and you'll see that most require no chopping at all. Both "prep" and "cook" times are listed so you can see just how quickly these dishes come together. More than 50 of the recipes are ready in 15 minutes or less and dozens use only five ingredients or less. These super-easy recipes are marked for quick identification.

How to Get the Most from Prepared Pasta Sauces

Prepared pasta sauces can play an important role in the quick cook's kitchen. Not only can you doctor them up to serve with pasta, you can use them as springboards for more inventive and impressive meals.

Which sauces are best? In researching this book and developing the recipes, I found literally hundreds of pasta sauces available in shelf-stable jars, cans, and refrigerated and frozen tubs. Dehydrated sauce mixes are also available, but these tend to be vastly inferior in quality when compared with refrigerated, frozen, and bottled sauces.

I wanted the ingredients in the book to be easily accessible by most consumers, so I focused on only the top four pasta sauces available in the marketplace: tomato sauce; pesto sauce; Alfredo sauce; and, to a lesser extent, cheddar cheese sauce. I researched supermarkets, gourmet stores, and online retailers to find the brands that are widely available. Then, I gathered neighbors, friends, and colleagues to sample dozens of sauces and find the best-tasting ones. Of course, I can't claim that we tasted everything. Many sauces are regional or local specialties and often come from restaurants in a particular city. For instance, in my region of eastern Pennsylvania, the local family-owned Italian restaurant Louie's makes Belletieri pesto and tomato sauces that are quite good. Other regions have their local favorites. I've focused mostly on brands that are available on a national level through supermarkets, gourmet stores, and online retailers.

The range of quality in these sauces is enormous. You can really taste the difference between a bottle of Ragu Tomato Basil Sauce ($1.29) and Rao's Homemade Tomato Basil Sauce ($7.99). Even though some tasters fondly associated less-expensive sauces with their childhood, they agreed that the pricier sauces tasted better. Most top-shelf pasta sauces are higher in price because they use high-quality, expensive ingredients.

Following is a brief review of widely available pasta sauces to help guide you through the sea of choices. It's not a comprehensive review by any means. For simplicity's sake, I grouped the sauces into three different tiers based on price. Tier 1 includes very widely distributed sauces that tend to be less expensive and use less-expensive ingredients (such as dried onions instead of fresh onions). Tier 2 contains middle-of-the-road sauces that are available in most markets, tend to cost a bit more, and use slightly more-expensive ingredients (such as extra-virgin olive oil instead of soybean oil). Tier 3 features premium sauces that carry the highest price tags, use high-quality ingredients (such as imported San Marzano tomatoes or basil from the Ligurian coast), and tend to be available only in regional markets or online. There are some good finds in each tier. Scoping out your favorite sauce is a matter of trying as many sauces as you can, deciding what you're willing to spend, and sticking with the flavors you like best.

What's in the Jar?

The first step in evaluating any pasta sauce is to look at the ingredients label. The ingredients can tell you a lot about the quality of the sauce. The best sauces use fresh ingredients rather than dried or dehydrated ones. Fresh garlic tastes noticeably better than garlic powder. If a prepared sauce starts with dried onions and dried garlic instead of fresh, there's only so much salt, sugar, fat, and "natural flavor" that can make it taste better. Look also for whole ingredients rather than pureed or reconstituted ones. Diced tomatoes usually have a more complex taste than do crushed tomatoes, tomato puree, or tomato paste. Avoid modified food starches and gums when possible. These ingredients thicken sauces inexpensively, but they can't match the texture of a sauce that has been simmered to evaporate excess moisture, concentrate its flavor, and naturally thicken its consistency.

When reading labels, keep in mind that ingredients are listed in order from highest concentration to lowest. If diced tomatoes are listed first, the sauce contains mostly diced tomatoes. If tomato puree is listed first, it contains mostly tomato puree. If water is listed first, you might want to look for another sauce.

Tomato Sauces

Scan the shelves of your typical grocery store and you'll be overwhelmed by the choices among tomato sauces, including marinara, arrabiata (with hot peppers), puttanesca (with olives and/or anchovies, capers, and hot peppers), tomato basil sauce, tomato vodka sauce, tomato sauce with red wine, with garlic and onion, with sun-dried tomatoes, with peppers, with mushrooms, with chunky garden vegetables, with spinach and cheese, with four cheeses, with meat, with sausage, and the list goes on. All of these varieties boil down to three basic tomato sauces: marinara, tomato basil, and tomato vodka sauce. The bulk of these sauces are sold in shelf-stable 26-ounce (737-g) glass jars in the pasta aisle or near the canned vegetables. But some brands of sauce, such as Buitoni, are sold refrigerated in 15-ounce (420-g) plastic tubs. Supermarkets usually stock the refrigerated sauces in low cases near the refrigerated pastas or near the cheese case.

If you're an online shopper, the choices among sauces widen considerably. You can buy Gia Russa Marinara Sauce for $12 a bottle, Williams-Sonoma Bolognese Sauce for $17 a bottle, and refrigerated Tomato Vodka Sauce directly from the renowned Legal Sea Foods restaurants. You'll also find scores of regional and hard-to-find imported pasta sauces. In this book, though, I've limited my reviews to brands that are widely available in supermarkets and gourmet stores around the country. Fortunately, these markets include some outstanding sauces such as Rao's Homemade.

MARINARA SAUCE AND TOMATO BASIL SAUCE.

Technically speaking, these are two different sauces. Marinara is traditionally a quickly made sauce including tomatoes, garlic, olive oil, oregano or basil, and salt (see page 20 for a recipe). Sometimes marinara is pureed smooth; sometimes it's left chunky. It's like Italian salsa: fresh, light, and bright tasting. Tomato-basil sauce, on the other hand, is more like gravy. It has a deeper, richer flavor and thicker texture. It's typically simmered longer to cook down the tomatoes and thicken the sauce (recipe on page 21). But in the world of jarred tomato sauces, there isn't much difference between the two. You can find a rich-tasting, chunky marinara alongside a weak and watery tomato basil sauce. It just depends on what name the manufacturer prefers.

Tier 1. This is the inexpensive group of tomato sauces that cost between $1.50 and $2.50 a bottle. Here you'll find the ubiquitous brands such as Ragu, Prego, Francesco Rinaldi, and Classico, as well as some store brands such as Master's Choice (A&P) and Wegman's. A quick look at the ingredients list will show why this tier of tomato sauces is so inexpensive. The first ingredient is usually tomato puree instead of diced tomatoes; these brands often use dried onions, dried garlic, and dried herbs instead of fresh; and soybean oil takes the place of olive oil. Sugar is added generously in the absence of ripe, fresh tomatoes. After sampling a range of these sauces, tasters chose Classico Sweet Basil Sauce as one of the standouts for the money. Compared with its peers, this sauce has more chunks of tomatoes, less tomato puree, and a noticeable glimmer of freshness.

Tier 2. These midrange sauces cost $3.00 to $4.50 a bottle and include such brands as Barilla, Emeril's, Newman's Own, Muir Glen, and Enrico's. Most tasters found that Muir Glen rose above the others in this group. You can taste the fresh onions, fresh tomatoes, extra-virgin olive oil, sweet basil, and—something not found in many other sauces—fennel. It's also organic. At roughly $3.89, it has the freshest, brightest taste of the lot. The slightly higher-priced Barilla brand ($4.19) came in as a close second runner-up.

Tier 3. Expect to pay between $5 and $12 a bottle for the cream-of-the-crop tomato sauces. This group includes Patsy's, Rao's Homemade, Mario Batali, Lidia's, Coco Pazzo, Victoria, Flora, Ventura, Coppola, and Bove's, among others. Buitoni refrigerated marinara sauce also falls into this category because of its high price tag—$4.99 for a 15-ounce (470-g) tub, or roughly $8.60 for the 26 ounces (737 g) found in your average jar. I didn't include Williams-Sonoma brand because it is so much costlier than the others ($17 a bottle). Regardless, it was hard to pick a favorite in this tier; tasters had good things to say about all of them. Eventually, Rao's rose to the top. The quality of Rao's imported tomatoes, imported olive oil, fresh onions, fresh garlic, and fresh basil gave it a bright, rich taste. You could almost taste the cast-iron pot in which the tomatoes were cooked. If you're looking for a bargain on the top shelf, Flora was a close second and cost only $4.99 compared with the $7.99 you'll pay for Rao's.

TOMATO VODKA SAUCE. Often served in restaurants with penne pasta, this tomato sauce variation is usually a smooth marinara-type sauce made with onions as well as garlic, a small amount of vodka, and a fair amount of cream that makes the sauce very rich, thick, and somewhat light in color (somewhere between pink and orange). Sometimes Parmesan cheese and prosciutto are added. For a recipe to make at home, see the variation of Quick Tomato Marinara Sauce on page 20.

Tier 1. Expect to pay only $1.50 to $2.50 here for brands such as Francesco Rinaldi "Super Premium Quality" Vodka Sauce. But don't get too excited. The first two ingredients of this brand's vodka sauce are tomato puree and cream cheese. The unconventional cream cheese makes this sauce unpleasantly thick. Other sauces at this price point tend to be disappointing as well. If you really like vodka sauce, try stepping up to Tier 2 at the least. It may simply be too expensive to make a sauce with cream and vodka at such a low price point.

Tier 2. $3.00 to $4.50. Bertolli, Emeril's, and Newman's Own fall into this group. Among these, Bertolli led the pack with Newman's Own close on its heels. Tasters enjoyed the rich texture, mild flavor, and chunks of tomato and onions in both brands.

Tier 3. $5.00 to $12.00. The top tier of vodka sauces includes Victoria, Bove's, Patsy's, Flora, and Rao's. Interestingly, neither Rao's nor Victoria vodka sauces contain cream, which is a typical ingredient. Instead, these brands use generous amounts of Parmesan and/or Romano cheese. Again, tasters found the flavor of Rao's to be the most compelling, even though its texture lacked the creaminess that usually defines vodka sauce. Patsy's was a bit creamier. But the overall taste and freshness of Rao's won out in the end.

Pesto Sauces

Basil pesto is a simple paste of basil leaves, pine nuts, garlic, Parmesan cheese, and olive oil. Changing the herbs, cheese, or proportion of ingredients varies the flavor and you'll find plenty of flavor variations in the marketplace. One of the most common is red pesto, made by adding sun-dried tomatoes (or tomato paste in the case of less-expensive brands). This sauce is so quick to make in a food processor that I encourage you to make mounds of fresh pesto when basil is plentiful in the summertime. Freeze it in tubs and you'll have pesto at the ready whenever you need it. A simple recipe appears on page 23.

In a pinch, you can find some refrigerated, jarred, and frozen pestos that are quite good. The best brands use only pine nuts in their pestos, but even some very good brands employ a mix of cashews and pine nuts. Others skimp by using dried basil instead of fresh. Imported brands that use fresh basil tend to taste better than domestic brands.

Look for jarred pestos near the pasta and bottled pasta sauces in your supermarket. If you can't find them there, head to the jarred roasted peppers or the condiment aisle, where some supermarkets stock their pesto. Refrigerated pesto sauces are usually sold in the refrigerated pasta case or in the cheese case. Because container sizes vary widely among pesto sauces, I've grouped the pestos below by price per ounce.

Tier 1. $0.25 to $0.65 per ounce. The least-expensive brands of pesto include Classico, DaVinci, Sacla, and Monterey Bay. Some of these producers use potatoes or potato flakes to thicken the sauce and give it body. Sunflower or soybean oil may stand in for olive oil to lower the cost. But you can still find a decent pesto here. In this tier, DaVinci had the freshest basil flavor and most agreeable texture. Sacla wasn't far behind, even though tasters found it a bit salty.

Tier 2. $0.70 to $0.99 per ounce. These midprice pestos include Roland, Flora, Victoria, and Buitoni (a refrigerated brand). Most in-store supermarket brands also fall into this price range (these tend be sold in bulk at the salad bar or olive bar of the market). There are two main characteristics that distinguish this group: fresh basil and extra-virgin olive oil, both of which are imported from Italy in the best brands. The standouts here are Victoria and Flora. Both of these basil pestos have a vivid green color and a rich aroma redolent of fresh basil leaves. Victoria came out ahead because it is less salty, which allows the fresh basil flavor to shine through.

Tier 3. $1.00 to $2.00 per ounce. Here you'll find brands such as Sole Mediterraneo, Rustichella D'Abruzzo, Alessi, Amore Concentrated Pesto Paste, and Whole in the Wall (sold frozen in tubs). Among these first-class pesto sauces, tasters found that Rustichella D'Abruzzo had the brightest taste and freshest basil aroma without being overly oily or salty. Whole in the Wall came in a close second.

Alfredo Sauce

Now we move into the dairy-based pasta sauces. According to Italian food authority John Mariani, the pasta dish fettuccine

Alfredo (or fettuccine alla panna) was created in 1914 by the Roman restaurateur Alfredo di Lelio. The sauce was originally a mixture of very rich homemade butter and Parmesan cheese thickened with flour. Most modern versions of Alfredo sauce dispense with the flour and use heavy cream instead. You can also find Alfredo sauce that features sun-dried tomatoes or other flavors. Due to the simplicity of the sauce and the preponderance of dairy products, Alfredo sauce is best made fresh. Plus, Alfredo sauce keeps refrigerated for days. Try the simple Alfredo sauce on page 24 for a homemade version.

Commercial varieties of Alfredo are available, but both refrigerated and jarred pale in comparison to fresh. Bottles of Alfredo are generally sold in 16-ounce (455-g) jars near the tomato pasta sauces in grocery stores. Refrigerated tubs are sold near the refrigerated pastas or in the cheese case.

Tier 1. $1.50 to $2.00 for 16 ounces (455 g). In the least-expensive category, you'll find such brands as Ragu Classic Alfredo. But at this price point, it's hard to create a delicious Alfredo sauce. As with vodka sauce, good-quality dairy products are crucial to success. If you like Alfredo sauce, my advice is to step up at least one tier.

Tier 2. $2.25 to $3.00 for 16 ounces (455 g). Bertolli and Classico dominate this tier, which also includes some low-calorie brands such as Walden Farms. These Alfredos often include egg yolks, gums, and other thickeners that aren't traditional. In this class, tasters found that Classico had the most agreeable texture, it isn't overly salty, and it features a handsome amount of black pepper that masks any "off" flavors.

Tier 3. $3.50 to $6.50 for 16 ounces (455 g). First-rate brands of Alfredo sauce are refrigerated to preserve the delicate freshness of the sauce. Popular brands such as Buitoni and DiGiorno appear alongside hard-to-find regional and local Alfredos made by restaurants. Among the widely distributed brands, Buitoni was the highest rated among tasters for its high proportion of butter, cream, and cheese with the least amount of additives. It's very rich (140 calories and 11 grams fat per ¼ cup, or 65 g), the way Alfredo sauce is supposed to be. It's also a bit less salty than DiGiorno.

Cheddar Cheese Sauce

Here's the sauce that flavors everyone's favorite macaroni and cheese. This pasta sauce is basically a white sauce (butter, flour, and milk) made with cheddar cheese and can be mixed up at home in less than 15 minutes. Because of its utter simplicity, I recommend that you make cheese sauce at home. The quality, even if you use subpar cheddar cheese, will outclass anything you can buy in a jar.

If you're in a bind, there is essentially only one brand of widely distributed cheddar cheese sauce for pasta: Ragu Double Cheddar.

Guide to Container Sizes

Whenever possible, I've tried to use whole containers of sauce in the recipes in this book. But sometimes 1 or 1 ½ cups (250 or 375 g) is all you need. Here's a guide to common container sizes for pasta sauces and how many cups you can expect from each. When storing leftover sauce, keep in mind that pesto keeps refrigerated for 1 to 2 weeks (or frozen for several months). Tomato sauces keep refrigerated for 4 to 5 days (or frozen for several months). Alfredo and cheddar cheese sauces will last 3 to 4 days in the refrigerator.

Sauce	Container Size	Volume Equivalent (approx.)
Tomato Basil, Marinara, or Vodka	26-ounce (737-g) jar	3 cups (750 g)
Tomato Basil, Marinara, or Vodka	15-ounce (420-g) refrigerated tub	1 ¾ cups (438 g)
Pesto	7-ounce (200-g) jar or tub	1 cup (260 g)
Pesto	10-ounce (280-g) jar	1 ⅓ cups (345 g)
Alfredo	16-ounce (455-g) jar	1 ¾ cups (438 g)
Alfredo	10-ounce (280-g) refrigerated tub	1 cup (250 g)
Cheddar Cheese	16-ounce (455-g) jar	1 ¾ cups (400 g)

which costs about $1.59 for a 16-ounce (455-g) jar. It's extremely mild in flavor and quite watery in texture, but you can improve it significantly by adding about 1 cup (112 g) real shredded cheddar cheese per cup of sauce used.

Using Homemade Sauces

The big question with prepared versus homemade pasta sauces is this: can you buy a refrigerated, jarred, or frozen sauce that's worth the price tag? In other words, will it be as good as or *better than* homemade?

In most cases, the answer is No. After having rated the best pasta sauces above, I have to confess that homemade sauces almost always taste better—as long as you start with good-quality ingredients. Maybe there's an incalculable pleasure that comes from making food yourself at home. But I suspect that it's just not physically possible for a sauce that is prepared, cooked, packaged, and shipped months in advance to reach the heights of flavor found in a freshly made sauce. Perhaps flavor is fleeting and best enjoyed in the few moments that it is directly in front of us.

If you're willing to go the extra mile for good food, consider this fact: the most popular pasta sauces take very little time to make. Honestly. Basil pesto is easily whirled in a food processor in less than 5 minutes (no cooking required). Alfredo sauce is merely butter, cream, and Parmesan cheese melted together in a saucepan (less than 8 minutes). Even tomato sauce can be made quickly. A good marinara sauce can be simmered in just 20 minutes with less than five ingredients. And a richly flavored tomato basil sauce simmers by itself for 40 minutes while you take care of other matters. When you can, treat yourself to the most satisfying food available by making these simple pasta sauces at home. Basic recipes for marinara, tomato basil sauce, Alfredo sauce, basil pesto sauce, cheddar cheese sauce, and countless variations appear starting on page 20.

Using Other Convenience Ingredients

Okay, sermon over. I know that most cooks want the best for less, so I've made every effort to simplify the recipes in this book by streamlining prep time whenever possible. I use convenience foods such as prechopped onions, prewashed lettuce leaves, and refrigerated or frozen prepared doughs. Here's a quick guide to these convenience foods.

Bacon. The recipes here call for various types of bacon, including Canadian bacon, pancetta (Italian unsmoked bacon), and thick slab bacon. To save time, some recipes call for precooked bacon. I'm not talking about fake bacon bits in a jar, but real bacon that is precooked and sold in strips or precrumbled in packs near the sliced bacon in most supermarkets. It needs only to be reheated and makes a fair substitute for freshly cooked bacon in a pinch. Hormel is a reliable brand.

Broth. If you don't make your own stock, concentrated broth bases are your best bet. Broth bases have a richer flavor than bouillon or canned broth, aren't as salty, and last for months in the refrigerator. Broth bases are usually sold in 8-ounce (225-g) jars in such popular brands as Better Than Bouillon and come in flavors from beef and chicken to vegetable and lobster. Just add a little water for a strong flavor or a lot of water for a gentle flavor. If you stock canned or boxed broths, try to use low-sodium varieties so you can control how much salt you add.

Cheese. For the best flavor, stick with block-style cheeses. When time is limited, however, use preshredded mozzarella, Monterey Jack, and other popular cheeses in the dairy aisle of your grocery store. Look for precrumbled feta and blue cheeses in the refrigerated cheese case or near the refrigerated hummus and refrigerated pasta. In the same case, you'll also find preshredded or preshaved *real* Parmesan, Romano, and Asiago cheese from such brands as DiGiorno in 5- to 6-ounce (140- to 170-g) tubs. These preshredded grating cheeses are much fresher tasting and have a much better texture than the "Parmesan" cheese sold in green canisters.

Dough. Using refrigerated and frozen pizza, bread, puff pastry, and pie doughs will save you loads of prep time in the kitchen. Refrigerated or frozen pizza dough is more versatile than fully cooked pizza crusts because you can shape the dough however you like, fill it to create such dishes as Ham and Cheese Calzones (page 183), or stuff it to make Deep-Dish Stuffed Sausage Pizza (page 164). Likewise, frozen puff pastry and phyllo dough shells take the fuss out of fancy appetizers. Just bake and fill. The same goes for prepared pie dough, which is now available in refrigerated sheets rather than frozen preformed pie crusts. The refrigerated sheets can be shaped into quiches, tarts, and pies of various sizes such as the Sun-Dried Tomato and Asparagus Quiche (page 239). Look for refrigerated pie dough near the other refrigerated prepared doughs and tortillas in your supermarket's dairy aisle.

Greens. Prewashed and pretrimmed spinach, arugula, and other salad mixes are a godsend for the busy cook. When you buy baby-size leaves, these greens don't even need to be chopped. Several recipes make use of these bagged greens to streamline prep time.

Precut produce. This huge category of new convenience foods has revolutionized the produce aisle. Alongside bagged salad, you can now buy tubs of fresh, prechopped, presliced, prediced, preshredded, and/or preminced onions, carrots, celery, and bell peppers. Some markets also carry frozen cut bell peppers and onions in the freezer case. Tired of peeling and mincing garlic and ginger? Buy preminced jarred garlic and ginger. If possible, go for the preminced garlic packed in oil rather than varieties packed in water. Oil-packed garlic retains better garlic flavor, and when the garlic is gone, you can use the garlic-flavored oil for cooking. Some brands of preminced garlic are sold in the produce aisle, while others can be found in the pasta and sauces section of supermarkets. Preminced ginger may be located near the minced garlic or in the Asian foods section.

Premarinated meats. A few recipes in this book use premarinated meats such as pepper-marinated pork tenderloin. These products are increasingly available in grocery store meat cases and offer obvious time savings. You can find premarinated legs of lamb; pork roasts, ribs, and chops; and turkey and chicken breasts and tenderloins in several popular flavors such as teriyaki, garlic and herb, and peppercorn.

Vegetable condiments. Jarred roasted red peppers, marinated artichoke hearts, brined capers, and oil-packed sun-dried tomatoes add bright bursts of flavor with very little effort. Oil-packed sun-dried tomatoes can be used right from the jar and are sold in halves, strips, and chopped bits, depending on your needs. Look for timesaving vegetable condiments like these in your supermarket's condiment aisle (near the ketchup and hot sauce), in the produce aisle, or in the pasta and pasta sauce section.

Wine. Not traditionally thought of as a convenience ingredient, wine is exactly that: flavor in a bottle. Keep some inexpensive ($8 to 10) reds and whites on hand for cooking. I use them most often to simmer in the pan after browning meats or sautéing vegetables. When the wine cooks down it concentrates in flavor, adding tremendous depth to simple pan sauces.

Quick Tomato Marinara Sauce

Marinara is a quickly made Italian-American tomato sauce. When pureed, it makes a great pizza sauce. Because it's made on the fly, canned tomatoes are commonly used. For this sauce, buy the best canned tomatoes available, such as San Marzano plum tomatoes. If the tomatoes aren't very red, ripe, and luscious, add ½ to 1 teaspoon sugar to balance the acidity of the tomatoes. In Italian, marinara means "mariner's style." As you might guess, this thin, fresh-flavored sauce is good with seafood. Some marinara sauces also include anchovies.

- ¼ cup (60 ml) extra-virgin olive oil
- 1 tablespoon (10 g) preminced oil-packed garlic
- 1 can (28 ounces, or 410 g) plum tomatoes in puree
- 3 tablespoons (12 g) chopped fresh basil or parsley or 1 teaspoon dried basil or oregano
   Salt and ground black pepper

Heat the oil in a large skillet or over medium heat. Add the onion and garlic and cook until lightly browned, 3 to 5 minutes. Working near the pan, pluck the tomatoes from the can one by one. Grab the firm stem end of each tomato and pinch and pull out the core from the tomato flesh. Discard the core and tear the flesh with your fingers, dropping tomato pieces into pan. Repeat with each tomato. Pour half of the canning liquid into the pan along with 2 tablespoons (8 g) of the basil or parsley (or all of the dried herbs). Bring to a boil, then reduce the heat to medium-low and cook until the tomatoes begin to break down, 10 to 15 minutes. For a thicker sauce, crush the tomatoes with a wooden spoon as they cook. Season to taste with salt and pepper. Stir in the remaining 1 tablespoon (4 g) basil or parsley. May be cooled and refrigerated in an airtight container for up to 2 days or frozen for up to 2 months.

Prep = 5 minutes   **Cook** = 20 minutes   **Yield** = About 3 cups (750 g)

Here are a few other popular variations:

- **Marinara Sauce with Red Wine:** Add ½ cup (60 ml) red wine after cooking the garlic and simmer until the liquid reduces in volume by about half.
- **Smooth Marinara Sauce:** After cooking, pass the mixture through a food mill or puree in the pan with a stick blender or in an upright blender or food processor.
- **Thick Marinara Sauce:** Stir in 2 tablespoons (30 g) tomato paste along with the tomatoes.
- **Spicy Marinara Sauce (Arrabiata):** Add ¼ to ½ teaspoon crushed red pepper flakes along with the garlic.
- **Tomato Vodka Sauce:** Sauté 1 cup (130 g) prechopped onion along with the garlic. After cooking, puree the mixture, add ¼ cup (60 ml) vodka, and bring to a boil. Reduce the heat to medium and simmer for 5 minutes. Reduce the heat to low and puree. Stir in ½ cup (240 ml) heavy cream, light cream, or half-and-half, and ½ cup (50 g) grated Parmesan cheese.

Simmered Tomato Basil Sauce

Spaghetti sauce is typically simmered longer than marinara sauce to deepen the flavors and thicken the texture. In this sauce, the sweetness of carrots cuts the acidity of tomatoes. Onions and celery round out the flavor base. Canned tomatoes are used for expediency here, but for the best taste, use fresh, ripe plum tomatoes (about 2½ pounds, or 1.1 kg, peeled, seeded, and chopped). To create

Prep = 7 minutes   **Cook** = 50 minutes   **Yield** = 4 cups (1000 g)

a richer flavor, add 1 cup (235 ml) red wine after sautéing the garlic and simmer the wine until reduced in volume by about half. Double the recipe if you like. The sauce will keep frozen for a couple of months.

> ¼ cup (60 ml) extra-virgin olive oil
> 1½ cups (195 g) prechopped onion
> ¾ cup (100 g) prechopped carrot
> ½ cup (80 g) prechopped celery
> 1 tablespoon (10 g) preminced oil-packed garlic
> 2 cans (28 ounces, or 785 g) plum tomatoes in puree
> 2 tablespoons (30 g) tomato paste (optional)
> ¼ cup (15 g) chopped fresh basil or 2 teaspoons dried
> Salt and ground black pepper

Heat the oil in a large, deep skillet or medium saucepan over medium heat. Add the onions, carrots, and celery, and cook until softened and lightly browned, 6 to 8 minutes. Add the garlic and cook 2 minutes. Working near the pan, pluck the tomatoes from the can one by one. For each tomato, grab the firm stem end of the tomato and pinch and pull out the core from the tomato flesh. Discard the core and tear the flesh with your hands, dropping the tomato pieces into the pan. Repeat with each tomato. Pour the liquid from one of the cans into pan. Stir in the tomato paste, if using, and 2 tablespoons (8 g) of the fresh basil (or all of the dried). Bring to a boil then reduce the heat to medium-low and simmer gently until the tomatoes break down and thicken and the sauce reduces in volume, 35 to 45 minutes. Season with salt and pepper and stir in the remaining fresh basil. For a smooth sauce, cool slightly and pass through a food mill or puree with a stick blender or in an upright blender or food processor.

May be cooled and refrigerated in an airtight container for up to 2 days or frozen for up to 2 months.

Other flavorful additions include:

- **Tomato Sauce with Mushrooms:** Add 8 ounces (225 g) presliced cremini or white mushrooms (about 2 cups) with the garlic and cook for 5 minutes.
- **Tomato Sauce with Roasted Red Peppers:** Add 1 cup (130 g) drained jarred roasted red peppers along with the tomatoes.
- **Tomato Sauce with Chunky Garden Vegetables:** Add 1 cup (130 g) prechopped bell peppers along with the onions. Add 4 ounces (115 g) (1 cup) presliced cremini or white mushrooms along with the garlic. If you like, add ¾ cup (75 g) chopped

zucchini about 15 minutes before the end of the simmering time. Do not puree.

- **Tomato Sauce with Spinach and Cheese:** Add 4 ounces (115 g) (about 2 cups) prewashed baby spinach leaves and ¾ cup (75 g) pregrated Parmesan cheese about 15 minutes before the end of the simmering time. Cook until the spinach wilts.
- **Tomato Sauce with Four Cheeses:** Add ½ cup (50 g) each pregrated Parmesan, pregrated Romano or Grana Padano, preshredded provolone, and ricotta cheese about 15 minutes before the end of the simmering time.
- **Tomato Sauce with Meat:** Add 12 ounces (340 g) lean ground beef and/or pork along with the garlic and cook until browned, 5 to 8 minutes, breaking up the meat with a spoon.
- **Tomato Sauce with Italian Sausage:** Add 12 ounces (340 g) mild or spicy Italian sausage (removed from casing if necessary) along with the garlic and cook until browned, 5 to 8 minutes, breaking up the meat with a spoon.

Basil Pesto Sauce

This fresh sauce takes mere minutes to make and it keeps frozen for months. Make it in the summer when fresh basil is bountiful. Freeze it in tubs, then simply scrape out what you need. It will taste better than anything you can buy in a jar. And it will thaw within a few minutes or, when mixed with anything hot, instantly.

> 10   cups (300 g) loosely packed fresh basil leaves
> 2   cups (200 g) pregrated Parmesan cheese
> ¾   cup (100 g) pine nuts
> 2   teaspoons pre-minced oil-packed garlic
> 1   teaspoon salt
> ¼   teaspoon ground black pepper
> ¾ to 1   cup (175 to 235 ml) extra-virgin olive oil

Put the basil, cheese, pine nuts, garlic, salt, and pepper in a food processor. Process until finely chopped, about 30 seconds. Scrape

Prep = 7 minutes   **Cook** = 50 minutes   **Yield** = 4 cups (1000 g)

down the sides of the processor bowl, then add ¾ cup (175 ml) of oil and blend to a loose paste, about 20 seconds, scraping the bowl as necessary. Add up to ¼ cup (60 ml) more oil for a looser, oilier pesto. Scrape into two small airtight containers and chill up to 1 week or freeze up to 8 months.

For an interesting variation, try:
- **Red Pesto Sauce:** Add ½ cup (25 g) oil-packed sun-dried tomatoes along with the basil.

Alfredo Sauce

Traditionally found on fettuccine, this quick sauce is ultrarich. If possible, use fresh (not ultrapasteurized) heavy cream and the best-quality Parmigiano-Reggiano you can find. Grate the cheese yourself for the freshest flavor. With so few ingredients, quality really counts here. Add a pinch of nutmeg if you like.

    6   tablespoons (84 g) butter
    1   cup (480 ml) heavy cream
    1   cup (100 g) freshly grated Parmesan cheese
        Salt and ground black pepper

Melt the butter in a large skillet over medium heat. Add the cream and bring just to a simmer, 2 to 3 minutes. Remove from the heat and stir in the Parmesan until melted and blended. Season with salt and black pepper. Use immediately. Or, cool and refrigerate for up to 1 day.
   Or, try this flavor variation:

- **Sun-Dried Tomato Alfredo Sauce:** Add ⅓ cup (16 g) finely chopped oil-packed sun-dried tomato bits along with the Parmesan.

Prep = 5 minutes   **Cook** = 50 minutes   **Yield** = 2 1/2 cups (375 g)

Cheddar Cheese Sauce

The taste of this easily made sauce will beat any jarred cheese sauce out there, especially if you use whole milk and good-quality cheddar cheese.

- 4 tablespoons (56 g) butter
- ¼ cup (30 g) all-purpose flour
- 2 cups (475 ml) milk, warmed in a microwave oven or small saucepan
- 1½ cups (6 ounces, or 170 g) shredded sharp cheddar cheese
- 1 teaspoon salt
- 1 teaspoon paprika
- 1 teaspoon Dijon mustard (optional)
- ⅛ teaspoon nutmeg (optional)
- ⅛ teaspoon ground black pepper

Melt the butter in a medium saucepan over medium heat. Whisk in the flour and cook for 1 to 2 minutes. Reduce the heat to medium-low and gradually whisk in 1 cup (235 ml) of the milk, whisking constantly to prevent lumps. Whisk in the remaining 1 cup (235 ml) milk and simmer gently, whisking frequently, until smooth and slightly thickened, about 5 to 8 minutes. Stir in the cheese, salt, paprika, mustard (if using), nutmeg (if using), and black pepper. Heat just until the cheese melts and the sauce is smooth.

Prep = 2 minutes   **Cook** = 13 minutes   **Yield** = 3 cups (690 g)

Beef Main Dishes

Parisian Bistro Steaks

Crispy oven french fries and steamed green beans complement this classic French dish—as does a goblet of red wine.

- 1 tablespoon (14 ml) olive oil
- 4 New York strip steaks, each about 10 ounces (280 g) and 1-inch (2.5-cm) thick
- ½ cup (120 ml) dry red wine
- 2 teaspoons preminced oil-packed garlic
- 2 teaspoons dried herbes de Provence
- 1 cup (250 g) refrigerated or jarred marinara sauce with red wine
- 2 tablespoons (8 g) chopped fresh parsley
   Salt and ground black pepper

In a large skillet, heat the oil over medium-high heat. Add the steaks. Cook until well browned, about 2 minutes per side. Off the heat, add the wine, garlic, and herbes. Return the pan to medium-high heat. Cook until the wine is reduced, about 3 minutes. Reduce the heat to medium-low and add the sauce. Stir into the wine reduction, turning the steaks to coat evenly. Cook until the steaks are medium-rare (about 145°F, or 60°C, on an instant-read thermometer), about 2 minutes. Sprinkle on the parsley. Season to taste with salt and pepper. Cut one of the steaks in half for two smaller portions, if you like.

Prep = 4 minutes **Cook** = 10 minutes **Yield** = 4 to 6 servings

Tenderloin Steaks with Blue Cheese Sauce

Elegant and sophisticated, yet oh-so-simple. Use whatever blue cheese you like—Gorgonzola, Cabrales, Roquefort, Stilton, Maytag—any one will do. No one but you will know the secret to your culinary success!

6	beef tenderloin steaks (about 5 ounces, or 140 g, each), 1-inch (2.5-cm) thick
	Salt and ground black pepper
1	tablespoon (14 g) butter
1	tablespoon (14 ml) olive oil
¼	cup (1 ounce, or 28 g) prechopped onion, minced
1	cup (250 g) refrigerated or jarred Alfredo sauce
½	cup (2 ounces, or 55 g) precrumbled blue cheese

Preheat the oven to 375°F (190°C, or gas mark 5). Have a heatproof platter on hand.

Season both sides of the steaks lightly with salt and pepper. In a large skillet, heat the butter and oil over medium-high heat. Add the steaks and cook until well browned, about 2 minutes per side. Remove to the platter and place the platter in the oven.

Add the onion to the skillet. Reduce the heat to medium-low. Cook, stirring, until golden, about 2 minutes. Add the sauce and cheese. Cook, stirring, until heated through, about 2 minutes. Keep warm over low heat.

Check the steaks with an instant-read thermometer for desired doneness: 145°F (60°C) for medium-rare; 160°F (70°C) for medium; 170°F (75°C) for well-done. Serve with the sauce.

Prep = 2 minutes   **Cook** = 12 minutes   **Yield** = 6 servings

Flank Steak
Spirals Pizzaiola

2   tablespoons (28 ml) olive oil, divided
1   bag (6 ounces, or 170 g) prewashed baby spinach
1   tablespoon (1 g) preminced oil-packed garlic
1   flank steak (1¾ to 2 pounds, or 795 g to 1 kg)
    Salt and ground black pepper
6   slices (5 ounces, or 140 g, total) sliced
    provolone cheese
6   slices (3 ounces, or 85 g, total) delicatessen
    baked ham
½   cup (120 ml) red wine, beef broth, or water
1½ cups (375 g) refrigerated or jarred tomato sauce
    with garlic and onion

Heat 1 tablespoon (14 ml) oil in a large skillet over medium-high heat. Add the spinach and garlic. Cook, tossing, until wilted, about 2 minutes. Set aside.

Place the flank steak on a cutting board. With a sharp knife, cut through the middle of the steak, parallel to the work surface, starting on one long side. Cut almost through to the other side. Open the steak like a book (it will be very thin). Patch any holes with thin slivers of the steak. Season lightly with salt and pepper. Lay the cheese, overlapping slightly, evenly over the surface. Lay the ham, overlapping slightly, evenly over the cheese. Cover with the spinach. Starting at one long end, roll into a tube. Tie with kitchen string or secure with toothpicks.

Heat the remaining 1 tablespoon (14 ml) oil in the pan over medium heat. Fry the steak roll, turning often, until completely browned, about 4 minutes. Add the wine, broth, or water, cooking a few minutes and scraping to remove browned bits from the pan. Add the sauce. Turn the roll to coat completely in sauce.

Cover and reduce the heat so the sauce is at a low simmer. Cook until the beef is very well done, about 30 minutes. Remove to a platter. Allow to rest for 10 minutes. Return any juices from the platter to the pan. Remove and discard the string or picks. Cut the roll into ½-inch-thick slices. Reheat the sauce and serve with the beef.

Prep = 10 minutes   **Cook** = 34 minutes, plus
10 minutes standing time   **Yield** = 4 to 6 servings

Beef and Potato Alfredo Kabobs

Beef tenderloin is more reliably tender
than sirloin, but you pay a higher price
for that tenderness. You make the choice.
Either way, the meat will be graced with a
velvety layer of creamy sauce during grilling.
Serve these with herbed rice.

- 8 small, round, red-skinned potatoes, cut into 1½-inch (4-cm) pieces
- 1 tablespoon (14 ml) olive oil
- 1 pound (455 g) beef tenderloin or sirloin steaks, cut into 1½-inch (4-cm) cubes
- 2 teaspoons steak-seasoning blend
- ¼ cup (15 g) chopped fresh parsley
- 1 tablespoon (14 ml) Worcestershire sauce
- 1 cup (250 g) refrigerated or jarred Alfredo sauce

Heat a grill to medium-high. Toss the potatoes and 1 teaspoon of the oil in a large microwaveable dish, cover, and microwave on high until the potatoes are just tender, about 4 minutes. Let cool. Add the beef cubes, steak seasoning, 2 tablespoons (8 g) of the parsley, and remaining 2 teaspoons oil to the bowl and toss to coat the beef and potatoes.

Arrange the beef and potatoes alternately on 4 skewers (about 4 pieces each for each skewer).

Mix the Worcestershire and 1 tablespoon (4 g) of the parsley with the Alfredo sauce in a medium bowl. Pour all but ¼ cup of the mixture into a small saucepan.

Brush the grill grate and coat with oil. Grill the skewers until the beef is browned all over and firm to the touch, 8 to 10 minutes, turning every 2 to 3 minutes. During the last 5 minutes of cooking, brush the skewers with the reserved ¼ cup Alfredo mixture from the bowl.

Simmer the Alfredo mixture in the saucepan on low until the flavors blend, about 5 minutes. Serve the skewers garnished with the remaining 1 tablespoon (4 g) parsley and the sauce on the side.

Prep = 10 minutes   **Cook** = 15 minutes   **Yield** = 4 servings

---

Spanish Skillet Picadillo

Fast enough for a weeknight supper, this skillet dinner adds Spanish flair to ground beef. Cooked rice and a tossed salad make perfect accompaniments. Or, serve the beef with warm tortillas for wrapping.

- 2 tablespoons (28 ml) olive oil
- 1 cup (4 ounces, or 130 g) prechopped onion
- 1 cup (4 ounces, or 130 g) prechopped tricolor bell pepper
- 1 tablespoon (10 g) preminced oil-packed garlic
- 1¾ pounds (795 g) ground beef
- 1 teaspoon ground black pepper
- ¼ teaspoon salt
- 1 cup (250 g) refrigerated or jarred marinara tomato sauce
- ⅓ cup (50 g) raisins
- ¼ cup (25 g) sliced pimento-stuffed Spanish olives

Heat the oil in a large skillet over medium heat. Add the onion, bell pepper, and garlic. Cover and cook, stirring occasionally, until golden, about 5 minutes. Scrape the vegetables to the side. Increase the heat to high. Crumble the beef into the pan. Season with pepper and salt. Cook, flipping and breaking the beef into small chunks, until the beef is no longer pink, about 5 minutes. Add the sauce, raisins, and olives. Reduce the heat to medium. Cook, stirring, until the mixture is bubbling, about 3 minutes.

Prep = 2 minutes   **Cook** = 13 minutes   **Yield** = 4-6 servings

Top-Secret Meatloaf

The time-honored trio of beef, cheddar, and rye bread come together in this distinctive loaf. Mashed potatoes and steamed broccoli complete this supreme comfort meal.

1½ pounds (680 g) ground round beef
1½ cups (75 g) coarsely crumbled day-old rye bread
1 cup (250 g) refrigerated or jarred cheddar cheese sauce, divided
¼ cup (1 ounce, or 28 g) prechopped onion, minced
1 egg, beaten
¼ cup (15 g) chopped fresh parsley
1 teaspoon ground black pepper

Preheat the oven to 350°F (180°C, or gas mark 4). Coat a 9 x 5 x 3-inch (22.5 x 13 x 7.5-cm) loaf pan with oil spray.

In a bowl, combine the beef, bread crumbs, ½ cup (125 g) sauce, onion, egg, parsley, and pepper. With hands, combine until well mixed. Transfer the mixture to the prepared pan. Smooth the top.

Bake until an instant-read thermometer inserted in the center registers 160°F (70°C), about 45 minutes. Let stand 15 minutes before slicing. Meanwhile, place the remaining ½ cup (125 g) sauce in a microwaveable dish. Cover with waxed paper. Cook on high power until heated, about 1 minute. Drizzle over each plated serving.

Prep = 5 minutes   **Cook** = 45 minutes, plus 15 minutes standing time   **Yield** = 4 to 6 servings

Pot Roast with Mushroom Cream

Most pot roasts are cooked with broth or other thin liquids that thicken slightly during cooking. This roast gets an extra boost of creaminess from Alfredo sauce.

1	beef chuck or bottom round roast (2½ to 3 pounds, or 1.1 to 1.5 kg)
1	teaspoon dried thyme
½	teaspoon ground black pepper
1	tablespoon (14 ml) olive oil
2	cups (260 g) prechopped onion
1	pound (455 g) presliced cremini or white mushrooms
1	tablespoon (10 g) preminced oil-packed garlic
1	cup (235 ml) dry sherry or white wine
1½ to 2	cups (355 to 475 ml) beef broth
1½	cups (375 g) refrigerated or jarred Alfredo sauce

Preheat the oven to 375ºF (190ºC, or gas mark 5).

Pat dry the roast with paper towels then rub all over with the thyme and black pepper.

Heat the oil in a Dutch oven or large ovenproof pot over medium-high heat. Add the meat and brown all over, about 8 minutes. Remove the meat to a platter. Add the onions and cook over medium heat until golden, about 4 minutes. Add the mushrooms and garlic and cook until the mushrooms give off their liquid, about 5 minutes. Pour in the sherry or white wine and scrape the pan bottom to loosen any browned bits. Return the meat to the pot with its juices and pour in enough broth to come about halfway up the meat.

Cover tightly and roast in the oven until the beef is fork-tender, about 2 hours. Add more broth as necessary to keep the liquid level about halfway up the meat. Remove the meat to a platter and cover. Skim excess fat from the surface of the liquid then stir in the Alfredo sauce and heat through over medium heat. Carve and serve with the sauce.

Prep = 15 minutes   **Cook** = 20 minutes
Yield = 4 servings

Meatballs in Brandied Gravy

Some markets sell "meatloaf mix,"
typically a combination of beef, pork,
lamb, and/or veal, which can be used for
meatballs as well. If you prefer pure beef, use
half ground chuck and half ground round. Serve
these meatballs with risotto or with fettucine tossed
with some extra Alfredo sauce.

- 1   slice white sandwich bread
- 2   cups (500 g) refrigerated or jarred Alfredo sauce
- 1½ pounds (680 g) ground beef, pork, and/or veal
- ½   cup (65 g) prechopped onion, minced
- 1   egg, beaten
- ½   teaspoon dried thyme
- ½   teaspoon ground black pepper
- ¼   cup (15 g) finely chopped fresh parsley
- 1   tablespoon (14 ml) olive oil
- 1   tablespoon (14 ml) brandy

Pulse the bread to coarse crumbs in a food processor or finely chop with a knife (about ½ cup, or 25 g, crumbs). Transfer to a medium bowl and stir in ½ cup (112 g) of the Alfredo. Stir in the meat, onion, egg, thyme, pepper, and 3 tablespoons (12 g) of the parsley. Using your hands, gently form into 1½-inch (4-cm) balls.

Heat half of the oil in a large skillet over medium heat. Add half of the meatballs and cook until browned all over, turning frequently, about 20 minutes. An instant-read thermometer inserted into the center of a meatball should register about 160ºF (70ºC). Repeat with remaining oil and meatballs.

Remove the meatballs to a deep platter or soup plates and cover with foil to keep warm. Add the brandy and 1 tablespoon (14 ml) water to the skillet. Cook, scraping the bottom of the pan, until the liquid nearly evaporates, 1 to 2 minutes. Reduce the heat to low and stir in the remaining 1½ cups (375 g) Alfredo. Cook until heated through, about 2 minutes, and pour over the meatballs. Garnish with the remaining 1 tablespoon (4 g) parsley.

Prep = 5 minutes   **Cook** = 40 minutes (mostly unattended)
Yield = 6 servings

Tex-Mex Pot Pie

Polenta may seem Italian, but corn-meal is also popular in the southwestern United States. Look for prepared polenta in the refrigerated produce section of your grocery store. Traditional flavor is fine, but if you can find polenta flavored with green chile and cilantro, that works best here.

2 teaspoons vegetable oil

1½ cups (195 g) prechopped onion

1 cup (120 g) prechopped bell peppers

¾ pound (340 g) ground beef

¾ pound (340 g) ground pork

1 tablespoon (9 g) chili powder

2 teaspoons preminced oil-packed garlic

1 cup (130 g) frozen corn

1 jar (26 ounces, or 730 g, about 3 cups) tomato sauce with chunky garden vegetables

1 package (16 ounces, or 455 g) refrigerated prepared polenta

1 cup (4 ounces, or 115 g) shredded pepper Jack cheese

Preheat the oven to 375ºF (190°C, or gas mark 5).

Heat the oil in a large skillet over medium-high heat. Add the onion and bell peppers. Cook, stirring occasionally, until softened, about 4 minutes. Scrape the vegetables to the side and crumble in the beef and pork. Add the chili powder and garlic and cook, flipping and breaking the meat into small chunks, until the meat is browned, about 5 minutes. Reduce the heat to medium-low and stir in the corn and sauce until heated through.

Scrape the mixture into a wide 3-quart (3-L) baking dish (such as 13 x 9-inch, or 33 x 23 cm). Slice the polenta into 12 rounds about ½-inch thick. Arrange the rounds over the meat mixture and sprinkle with the cheese.

Bake until the filling is bubbly and the cheese is lightly browned, 25 to 30 minutes.

Prep = 5 minutes **Cook** = 2 to 2½ hours (mostly unattended)
Yield = 6 to 8 servings

Shredded Beef Burritos

Cubed beef chuck is an inexpensive cut that takes well to slow cooking. As the cubes cook unattended, the connective tissue in the meat dissolves, moistening the meat and creating a luscious sauce. The cubes make a great alternative to ground beef for burritos and tacos, offering a bit more chew and better overall texture.

1	pound (455 g) cubed beef chuck (1½-inch, or 4-cm, cubes)
1	tablespoon (9 g) chili powder
1	tablespoon (14 ml) olive oil
2	teaspoons preminced oil-packed garlic
1	bay leaf
1	cup (235 ml) beef broth
1 to 1½	cups (250 to 325 g) refrigerated or jarred tomato sauce with garlic and onion
8	(8-inch) flour tortillas, warmed
¾	cup (98 g) prechopped onion, finely chopped
1	cup (4 ounces, or 115 g) shredded pepper Jack cheese

Pat dry the beef cubes with paper towels, then rub with the chili powder. Heat the oil in a large, deep skillet or wide saucepan over medium-high heat. Add the beef and cook until browned all over, 3 to 5 minutes. Add the garlic and bay leaf and cook for 1 minute. Add the stock and boil for 1 minute, scraping the bottom of the pan to loosen any browned bits. Stir in just enough of the sauce to barely cover the beef. Reduce the heat to low, cover and simmer until the beef is fork tender and easy to shred, 1½ to 2 hours.

Using a slotted spoon, remove the beef to a bowl and discard the bay leaf. Tear the beef into shreds with a fork. Add about 1/2 cup of the sauce from the pan. Roll up about ⅓ cup of the filling in a tortilla and garnish with some of the onion, remaining sauce, and cheese.

Prep = 5 minutes **Cook** = 1½ hours
(mostly unattended) **Yield** = 4 servings

Sweet and Sour Braised Brisket

Like many slow-cooked dishes, this one tastes best the next day. To serve it that way, let the meat cool to room temperature, then refrigerate it overnight. Reheat the next day and serve with potatoes or noodles and roasted or steamed vegetables. To make this dish in a slow-cooker, put all of the ingredients into the slow-cooker, and cook on low for 10 hours or on high for 4 to 5 hours.

1   first-cut or thin-cut beef brisket (about 4 pounds, or 2 kg)
2   teaspoons lemon-pepper seasoning
1   tablespoon (14 ml) vegetable oil
3   cups (390 g) prechopped onion
½ to 1 cup (120 to 235 ml) beef broth
1½   cups (375 g) refrigerated or jarred marinara tomato sauce with red wine
½   cup (120 ml) apple cider vinegar
½   cup (110 g) light brown sugar
1   bay leaf

Preheat the oven to 350°F (180°C, or gas mark 4). Pat dry the brisket, then rub with the lemon-pepper.

Heat the oil in a Dutch oven or other large ovenproof pot over medium-high heat. When hot, add the brisket and brown all over, about 5 minutes per side. Remove the meat to a platter and cover with foil to keep warm.

Add the onions to the pan and cook until golden, about 4 minutes, stirring frequently. Add ½ cup (120 ml) of the broth, scraping the pan bottom to loosen any browned bits. Stir in the sauce, vinegar, brown sugar, and bay leaf. Return the brisket to the pan with its juices and spoon some sauce over it. Cover tightly and roast in the oven until fork-tender, 2½ to 3 hours. If necessary, add additional broth to keep the liquid level about halfway up the meat. Remove the brisket to a platter and let cool for 5 to 10 minutes.

Carve the brisket against the grain into ½-inch thick slices. Serve with the sauce.

Prep = 5 minutes **Cook** = 2 to 3 hours
(mostly unattended) **Yield** = about 8 servings

Braised Chipotle Chuck Roast

Here's the perfect supper for those who like their beef with spicy attitude. For more timid palates, serve cooked rice on the side as a buffer from the heat.

1	beef chuck roast (2 to 2½ pounds, or 1 to 1.1 kg)
2	teaspoons ground chipotle chile
1	tablespoon (14 ml) olive oil
2	tablespoons (20 g) preminced oil-packed garlic
1½	cups (375 g) refrigerated or jarred tomato sauce with chunky vegetables
12	ounces (340 g, or 2½ cups) tomatillos or green tomatoes, chopped
8	ounces (225 g, or 2 cups) zucchini cut into ½-inch chunks
1	cup (5 ounces, or 140 g) baby carrots
½	cup (30 g) chopped fresh cilantro

Preheat the oven to 375°F (190°C, or gas mark 5).

Pat dry the meat with paper towels then sprinkle all over with the ground chipotle.

Heat the oil in a Dutch oven or other large ovenproof pot over medium-high heat. Add the meat to the pot and brown all over, about 8 minutes. Remove the meat to a platter and cover to keep warm. Add the garlic and cook 1 minute. Remove from the heat and stir in the sauce, tomatillos or green tomatoes, zucchini, and carrots. Return the roast to the pot with its juices, spooning some of the sauce over the roast.

Cover tightly. Roast in the oven until the beef is fork-tender, about 2 hours. Remove the roast to a platter and cover to keep warm. Skim excess fat from the surface of the liquid then stir in the cilantro. Carve the roast and serve with the sauce.

Prep = 10 minutes **Cook** = 2 hours **Yield** = 6 servings

Braised Beef Short Ribs

For the most flavor, look for short ribs cut from the chuck (shoulder) of the steer. Most markets sell English-style short ribs, which look like a rectangular block of meat and bone. Or, you could use flanken-style short ribs, but the bones are shorter in this cut, so it's harder to get the meat off the bones.

3½ to 4	pounds (1.5 to 2 kg) bone-in beef short ribs
1½	teaspoons crushed dried rosemary
½	teaspoon ground black pepper
2	tablespoons (28 ml) olive oil
2	cups (260 g) prechopped onion
8	ounces (225 g) presliced cremini or white mushrooms
2	tablespoons (20 g) preminced oil-packed garlic
1	cup (235 ml) red wine
1½	cups (375 g) refrigerated or jarred marinara tomato sauce with red wine
1 to 1½	cups (235 to 355 ml) beef broth

Preheat the oven to 350°F (180°C, or gas mark 4).

Pat dry the short ribs with paper towels then rub all over with the rosemary and black pepper.

Heat the oil in a Dutch oven or other large ovenproof pot over medium-high heat. When hot, add the short ribs (in batches if necessary) and brown all over, 10 to 15 minutes. Remove the meat to a platter and cover with foil to keep warm.

Prep = 5 minutes **Cook** = 2½ to 3 hours (mostly unattended)
Yield = 4 to 6 servings

Pour off all but 2 tablespoons (28 ml) of the fat and reduce the heat to medium. Add the onions to the pan and cook until golden, about 4 minutes, stirring frequently. Add the mushrooms and garlic and cook until the mushrooms give off their liquid, about 4 minutes. Add the wine and bring to a simmer over medium-high heat, scraping the pan bottom to loosen any browned bits. Cook until the liquid is reduced to about ½ cup (120 ml).

Return the short ribs to the pot and pour in the sauce and enough broth (if necessary) so that the liquid comes about halfway up the meat. Bring to a simmer then cover tightly.

Roast in the oven until the meat is fork-tender and pulls away easily from the bones, 2 to 2½ hours. Add additional broth as necessary to keep the liquid level about halfway up the meat. Remove the ribs to a platter and cover to keep warm. Skim excess fat from the surface of the pan, then simmer the braising liquid over medium-high heat until thick like gravy. Serve the ribs with the sauce.

Pesto Crusted
Stuffed Beef Tenderloin

Save this recipe for a special occasion. The meat is expensive, but, oh so worth it. If you can find it, use a center-cut tenderloin roast, known as Chateaubriand. Or, if your tenderloin roast is cut from the end and has a tapering "tail" of meat on it, tuck the tail underneath so the meat is of even thickness, and tie it securely in several places with kitchen string. To easily make the bread crumbs for this dish, pulverize one slice of sandwich bread to crumbs in a food processor.

- 1 center-cut beef tenderloin roast (about 3 pounds, or 1.5 kg), trimmed and tied if necessary
- ½ cup (25 g) oil-packed sun-dried tomato strips or bits
- ½ cup (65 g) frozen corn, thawed
- ½ cup (25 g) fresh breadcrumbs
- ⅓ cup (30 g) pregrated Parmesan cheese
- 2 scallions, finely chopped
- 3 tablespoons (24 g) pine nuts
- 1 egg, lightly beaten
- 1 tablespoon (4 g) chopped fresh parsley
- ½ cup (130 g) refrigerated or jarred basil pesto

Prep = 10 minutes   **Cook** = 40 minutes   **Yield** = 6 servings

Preheat the oven to 500°F (250°C, or gas mark 10).

Make a hole down the center of the tenderloin by positioning a sharpening steel or the handle of a long wooden spoon at the thicker end of the tenderloin. Push the steel or spoon handle through until the tip comes out the other side, then remove. Insert a long, thin-bladed knife into the hole, making short slits to enlarge the hole.

In a medium bowl, combine the sun-dried tomatoes, corn, bread crumbs, cheese, scallions, pine nuts, egg, and parsley.

Stand the tenderloin on end and spoon the stuffing into the hole, pushing it through with the steel or spoon handle. When half of the stuffing is in the meat, invert the tenderloin and fill the hole from the other side.

Pat dry the surface of the meat with paper towels and put the meat on a rack in a roasting pan. Rub the entire surface with the pesto. (At this point, the meat can be refrigerated for up to 4 hours if necessary; let the meat rest at room temperature for 30 minutes before roasting.)

Roast until well browned all over, 15 to 20 minutes. Reduce the oven temperature to 325°F (170°C, or gas mark 3) and roast until an instant-read thermometer inserted into the meat (but not the center) registers 120°F (50°C) for medium-rare, 20 to 25 minutes more. Remove from the oven, cover loosely with foil, and let rest for 10 to 15 minutes. Slice about ½-inch thick.

Pan-Seared Steaks with Spicy Tomato Sauce

Botanically speaking, sweet bell peppers are a mild form of chile. Here, they're paired with dried and ground ancho and smoky-hot chipotle chile powders.

- 2 tablespoons (14 g) paprika
- 1 tablespoon (18 g) kosher salt
- 1 tablespoon (6 g) ground ancho chile
- 2 teaspoons light brown sugar
- 1 teaspoon ground chipotle chile
- ½ teaspoon ground cumin
- ½ teaspoon ground black pepper
- 4 rib-eye beef steaks, each about 10 ounces (280 g) and ¾-inch thick
- 1 cup (130 g) prechopped onion
- 1 cup (130 g) prechopped bell peppers
- 1¼ cup (300 g) refrigerated or jarred tomato sauce with red peppers

Mix together the paprika, salt, ancho, brown sugar, chipotle, cumin, and black pepper. Rub half of the mixture over the steaks.

Heat a large skillet over medium-high heat. When hot, add the steaks and cook until the steaks are medium-rare (about 145ºF, or 60ºC, on an instant-read thermometer), 3 to 5 minutes per side. Remove to a platter or plates and cover with foil to keep warm.

Add the onion, bell peppers, and remaining spice mix to the skillet. Cook, stirring frequently, until the vegetables are beginning to soften, 3 to 4 minutes. Add the tomato sauce and reduce the heat so that the mixture simmers gently. Simmer until the flavors have blended, about 5 minutes. Serve with the steaks.

Prep = 7 minutes **Cook** = 15 minutes **Yield** = 4 servings

Pork Main Dishes

Yucatan-Style
Shredded Pork

The enticing flavors of this stew improve
with age, so feel free to prepare it several days
in advance. It freezes well, too. Serve with
corn tortillas or rice.

2	tablespoons (28 ml) olive oil
2	bunches scallions, all parts, cut into 1-inch (2.5-cm) pieces (1½ cups, or 150 g)
1	tablespoon (10 g) preminced oil-packed garlic
1	cup (250 g) refrigerated or jarred tomato sauce with garlic and onion
¼ to ½	cup (55 to 110 g) jarred or canned green chile salsa, divided
½	teaspoon ground cumin
1	boneless pork shoulder roast, Boston butt (1¾ to 2 pounds, or 795 g to 1 kg)

Preheat the oven to 325°F (170°C, or gas mark 3).

In a large ovenproof pot set over medium-high heat,
combine the oil, scallions, and garlic. Cook, stirring, until
fragrant, about 2 minutes. Add the sauce, ¼ cup (55 g) salsa,
and cumin. Cook, stirring, until hot, about 2 minutes. Place
the pork in the pot, spooning some sauce over it. Cover
tightly.

Bake until the pork is fork tender, about 1½ hours. Use a
fork to pull the pork into shreds at the table and pass with
the remaining ¼ cup (55 g) salsa.

Prep = 5 minutes   **Cook** = 1 hour 30 minutes
Yield = 4 to 6 servings

Sausages with White Beans and Tomatoes

Think of this dish as uptown franks and beans. The franks are the main focus, so buy the best sausages you can find. If you like, add some herbs (fresh or dried) such as dried rosemary or thyme along with the mushrooms. For a more substantial meal, serve this over pasta that's tossed with a little extra tomato sauce.

- 1½ pounds (680 g) fresh pork sausage links (mild or spicy)
- ¼ cup (33 g) prechopped onion
- 4 ounces (115 g) presliced cremini or white mushrooms
- 2 cups (500 g) refrigerated or jarred tomato sauce with garlic and onion
- 1 can (16 ounces, or 455 g) small white beans, rinsed and drained

Heat a medium saucepan over medium-high heat. Add the sausages and prick them in a few places with a fork. Cook until well-browned all over, 15 to 20 minutes. Remove to a plate and let cool slightly.

Add the onions to the pan and cook until golden, about 4 minutes. Reduce the heat to medium, add the mushrooms, and cook until they give up their liquid, about 4 minutes. Add the tomato sauce and reduce the heat to medium-low.

Cut the sausages in half lengthwise, then crosswise into half-moon shapes. Return to the sauce along with the beans. Simmer gently for 5 to 10 minutes.

Prep = 2 minutes   **Cook** = 30 minutes   **Yield** = 4 servings

Skillet Pork and Chickpeas in Red Pesto Sauce

This dish is so fast and tasty, it's bound to become a weeknight favorite. Turkey breast or chicken thighs can take the place of the pork. Serve with noodles, rice, or risotto.

- 2 tablespoons (28 ml) olive oil
- ½ cup (65 g) prechopped onion
- ½ cup (65 g) baby carrots, cut into ¼-inch chunks
- ½ cup (80 g) prechopped celery
- 2 teaspoons preminced oil-packed garlic
- 1¼ pounds (570 g) cubed pork
- 1 can (15 ounces, or 420 g) chickpeas, rinsed and drained
- 5 tablespoons (80 g) jarred or refrigerated red pesto sauce

Heat the oil in a large skillet set over medium-high heat. Add the onion, carrot, celery, and garlic. Cook, stirring occasionally, until golden, about 4 minutes. Scrape the vegetables to the side. Add the pork. Cook for about 4 minutes, turning frequently, until browned on all sides. Add the chickpeas. Cook, stirring occasionally, until the pork is cooked through, about 5 minutes. Remove from the heat. Stir in the pesto sauce.

Prep = 2 minutes   **Cook** = 13 minutes   **Yield** = 4 to 6 servings

Chipotle Pork Medallions

Simple, smoky, and spicy, these pork medallions make a great presentation. Garnish with chopped fresh cilantro.

- 1 pork tenderloin (about 1¼ pounds, or 570 g)
- 1 tablespoon (6 g) ground chipotle chile
- 2 tablespoons (28 ml) olive oil
- ½ cup (120 ml) chicken broth
- 1½ cups (375 g) refrigerated or jarred tomato sauce with garlic and onion

Slice the pork crosswise into ¼-inch-thick medallions. Dust all over with the chipotle chile.

Heat the oil in a large skillet over medium-high heat. Add the pork (in batches, if necessary) and cook, turning once, until the pork is no longer pink, 2 to 3 minutes per side. Transfer the pork to a platter and cover with foil to keep warm.

Add the broth to the pan and boil, scraping the pan bottom. Reduce the heat to medium and stir in the sauce and any pork juices from the platter. Simmer for 5 minutes. Serve over the pork.

Prep = 5 minutes **Cook** = 10 minutes **Yield** = 4 servings

5 INGREDIENTS OR LESS

15 MINUTES OR LESS

Pork Medallions with Port Cream

Look for premarinated pork tenderloin in your supermarket's meat case. Garnish the blush-colored sauce with chopped fresh parsley.

- 1 premarinated peppercorn pork tenderloin (about 1¼ pounds, or 570 g)
- 2 teaspoons paprika, sweet or smoked
- 2 tablespoons (28 ml) olive oil
- ¾ cup (175 ml) ruby port
- 1 cup (250 g) refrigerated or jarred Alfredo sauce
  Parsley, for garnish

Slice the pork crosswise into ¾-inch-thick medallions. Dust all over with the paprika.

Heat the oil in a large skillet over medium-high heat. Add the pork (in batches, if necessary) and cook, turning once, until the pork is no longer pink, 2 to 3 minutes per side. Transfer the pork to a platter and cover with foil to keep warm.

Add the port to the pan and boil, scraping the pan bottom, until the liquid is reduced by about half. Reduce the heat to medium-low and stir in the sauce and any pork juices from the platter. Heat through for 5 minutes. Serve over the pork and garnish with the parsley.

Prep = 5 minutes   **Cook** = 10 minutes   **Yield** = 4 servings

5 INGREDIENTS OR LESS

15 MINUTES OR LESS

Hungarian Pork Cutlets in Creamy Paprika Sauce

If you like spice but not too much heat, here's a mildly seasoned super-quick main dish. Serve it with buttered egg noodles and sautéed green beans.

- 1   tablespoon (14 g) butter
- ½ cup (65 g) prechopped onion, minced
- 6   thin boneless loin pork chops
      (about 1½ pounds, or 570 g)
- 2   teaspoons paprika
- 1   cup (250 g) refrigerated or
      jarred Alfredo sauce

Melt the butter in a large skillet over medium-high heat. Add the onion and cook until golden, stirring occasionally, 2 to 3 minutes. Pat dry the cutlets and sprinkle with the paprika. Scrape the onion to the side of the pan and increase the heat to high. Add the cutlets and cook until browned, about 1 minute per side. Add the sauce and stir to coat the chops. Reduce the heat to medium-low and simmer until the pork is no longer pink, about 3 minutes.

Prep = 2 minutes   **Cook** = 8 minutes
Yield = 4 to 6 servings

5 INGREDIENTS OR LESS

15 MINUTES OR LESS

Lemon Pesto Pork Cutlets

Thin boneless pork chops cook so quickly that they're tailor-made for fast weeknight meals. Garnish the cutlets with chopped fresh basil and serve with lemon wedges for squeezing.

- 1 tablespoon (14 g) butter
- 6 thin boneless loin pork chops (about 1¼ pounds, or 570 g)
- 2 teaspoons lemon-pepper seasoning
- ½ cup (120 ml) white wine or low-sodium chicken broth
- ¾ cup (195 g) refrigerated or jarred basil pesto

Melt the butter in a large skillet over medium-high heat. Pat dry the cutlets and coat all over with the lemon pepper. Add to the pan and cook until browned, about 1 minute per side. Add the wine or broth to the pan, stir, and simmer until the wine reduces in volume slightly, 1 to 2 minutes. Reduce the heat to medium-low and simmer until the pork is no longer pink, 1 to 2 minutes. Remove the cutlets to a platter or plates and cover to keep warm. Stir the pesto into the pan. Serve the sauce over the cutlets.

Prep = 2 minutes   **Cook** = 8 minutes   **Yield** = 4 to 6 servings

Pork Chops in Provençal Tomato Sauce

If you skip chopping the olives here (which you can do with smaller olives), this recipe requires absolutely no chopping at all.

- 1 tablespoon (14 ml) olive oil
- 6 boneless loin pork chops (about 2 pounds, or 1 kg, total)
  Salt and ground black pepper
- ½ cup (65 g) prechopped onion
- 1 tablespoon (10 g) preminced oil-packed garlic
- 2 teaspoons dried herbes de Provence or rosemary
- 1 cup (250 g) refrigerated or jarred marinara tomato sauce with red wine
- 2 tablespoons (16 g) chopped oil-cured black olives

Heat the oil in a large skillet set over high heat. Pat dry the chops and lightly season with salt and pepper. Add to the skillet and cook until browned, about 2 minutes per side.

Remove the pork chops to a platter. Reduce the heat to medium and add the onions, garlic, and herbes de Provence or rosemary. Cook until the onions are golden, about 4 minutes. Add the sauce, olives, and pork chops with the juices from the platter. Cover and cook at a low simmer until the pork is no longer pink, about 4 minutes.

Prep = 3 minutes   **Cook** = 12 minutes   **Yield** = 4 to 6 servings

Pork Chops in Fennel Sauce

Once totally foreign, Florence fennel is now a commonplace vegetable in supermarket produce sections. Look for bulbs that are firm and pale green with no sign of browning. The dark lacy leaves can be chopped and used as a fresh herb.

1 bulb fennel (about 1 ¼ pounds, or 570 g)
1 tablespoon (14 ml) olive oil
6 boneless pork chops (about 2 pounds, or 1 kg, total)
   Salt and ground black pepper
2 tablespoons water
1 cup (250 g) refrigerated or jarred marinara tomato sauce
1 navel orange, cut into wedges

Remove and discard the fibrous light-green stems from the fennel bulb. Reserve 2 tablespoons (8 g) dark-green feathery leaves. Quarter the white bulb and cut into ¼-inch thick slices.

Heat the oil in a large skillet set over high heat. Pat dry the chops and lightly season with salt and pepper. Add to the skillet and cook until browned, about 2 minutes per side. Remove the pork chops to a platter.

Reduce the heat to medium and add the sliced fennel and water to the pan. Scrape the pan bottom to remove browned bits. Cover and cook until the pan is dry and the fennel starts to brown, about 3 minutes. Add the sauce and pork chops with their juices from the platter. Cover and cook at a low simmer until the pork is no longer pink, about 4 minutes. Sprinkle on the reserved fennel leaves. Serve with the orange wedges.

Prep = 3 minutes   **Cook** = 12 minutes
Yield = 4 to 6 servings

Baked Pork Chops
with Mushrooms

Slow baking in liquid is a foolproof method for making tender pork chops. Despite the long cooking time, the hands-on time here is only about 10 minutes. Then the chops bake on their own while you do something else.

6   bone-in pork loin chops, at least 1-inch (2.5-cm) thick (about 3 pounds, or 1.4 kg, total)
1½ teaspoon dried thyme
½   teaspoon salt
⅛   teaspoon ground nutmeg
¼   teaspoon ground black pepper
1   tablespoon (14 ml) olive oil
1   pound (455 g) presliced cremini or white mushrooms
2   teaspoons preminced oil-packed garlic
1   cup (235 ml) dry white wine
1   cup (250 g) refrigerated or jarred Alfredo sauce

Preheat the oven to 325ºF (170°C, or gas mark 3).
    Pat dry the chops and coat all over with the thyme, salt, nutmeg, and black pepper.
    Heat the oil in a large skillet over medium-high heat. Add the chops and fry until browned, about 2 minutes per side. Remove the chops to a 13 x 9-inch (32.5 x 22.5-cm) baking dish.
    Add the mushrooms to the skillet and cook over medium-high heat until they give up their liquid, 3 to 4 minutes. Add the garlic and cook 1 minute. Add the wine and simmer, scraping the pan bottom, for 1 minute. Reduce the heat to low and stir in the Alfredo sauce.
    Pour the mixture over the pork chops and cover tightly with a double layer of foil. Bake until the chops are fork tender, 2 to 2½ hours.

Prep = 3 minutes   **Cook** = 2 ½ hours (mostly unattended)
Yield = 6 servings

Roasted Pork Tenderloin with Red Pesto Crust

Perfect for company, this dish goes into the oven for 45 minutes while you tend to other matters.

- 2 pints (600 g) grape tomatoes
- 2 medium zucchini, coarsely chopped
- 1 tablespoon (10 g) preminced oil-packed garlic
- 2 tablespoons (28 ml) olive oil
- ½ teaspoon salt
- ½ teaspoon ground black pepper
- 3 pounds (1.5 kg) premarinated peppercorn pork tenderloin
- ¾ cup (195 g) refrigerated or jarred red pesto sauce

Preheat the oven to 375°F (190°C, or gas mark 5).

Mix the tomatoes, zucchini, garlic, oil, salt, and pepper in a 17 x 11-inch (42.5 x 27.5-cm) baking dish until coated with oil. Brush the tenderloins all over with the pesto, then nestle them into the pan about 4 inches (10 cm) apart.

Roast until the juices run clear (155°F, or 70°C) on an instant-read thermometer inserted into the center), about 45 minutes. Let stand for 10 minutes. Slice and serve with the vegetables.

Prep = 5 minutes **Cook** = 45 minutes (all unattended)
Yield = 8 servings

Tenderloin and Chorizo Enchiladas

Wrapped in corn tortillas and topped with spicy tomato sauce, this beef and pork filling makes a satisfying main course. If you prefer, replace the chipotle peppers with a drained can of sliced jalapeños (about 4 ounces, or 115 g).

8	(6-inch) corn tortillas
1	pound (455 g) premarinated peppercorn pork tenderloin, halved lengthwise
½	teaspoon ancho chili powder
½	teaspoon ground cumin
½	teaspoon dried oregano
2	teaspoons olive oil
6	ounces (170 g) fresh Mexican chorizo, casing removed
1	tablespoon (10 g) preminced oil-packed garlic
1¼	cup (300 g) refrigerated or jarred tomato sauce with garlic and onion
2 to 3	canned chipotle chiles in adobo sauce
2	teaspoons chipotle canning liquid
¼	cup (60 ml) water or chicken broth
4	ounces (115 g, or 1 cup) shredded pepper Jack cheese

Prep = 15 minutes   **Cook** = 30 minutes
Yield = 4 servings

Preheat the oven to 350°F (180°C, or gas mark 4). Wrap the stack of tortillas in foil and bake for 10 minutes.

Meanwhile, coat the pork all over with the chili powder, cumin, and oregano. Heat the oil in a large skillet over medium-high heat. Add the pork and cook until browned on all sides and slightly pink in the middle, 4 to 6 minutes. Remove to a clean cutting board, let rest 5 minutes, then slice thinly.

Add the chorizo to the skillet and cook over medium heat until browned, breaking up the meat, about 5 minutes. Add the garlic and heat through 1 minute. Remove from the heat and stir in the pork slices.

Puree the tomato sauce, chipotle chiles and canning liquid in a food processor or blender with ¼ cup (60 ml) water or chicken broth. Spread a thin layer of the sauce over the bottom of an 11 x 7-inch (27.5 x 17.5-cm) or other 1½-quart (1.5-L) baking dish.

Sprinkle about a tablespoon (7 g) of the cheese and ⅓ cup of the pork mixture in a column down the center of each tortilla. Roll up and arrange seam-side down in the baking dish. Top evenly with the remaining sauce and cheese. Bake until hot and bubbly, 15 to 20 minutes.

Polynesian Pork Roast

Have a luau in your kitchen with this
easy oven main course. Serve with cooked
rice and chopped macadamia nuts for a
summertime meal.

1½ cups (6 ounces, or 170 g) prediced tricolored bell peppers
1½ cups (6 ounces, or 170 g) prechopped onion
1   cup (8 ounces, or 225 g) drained canned or refrigerated
    pineapple chunks in juice
1   cup (250 g) refrigerated or jarred marinara tomato sauce
½   cup (120 ml) water
¼   cup (50 g) brown sugar
2   tablespoons (16 g) refrigerated pregrated fresh ginger
2   teaspoons hot pepper sauce
1   boneless pork loin roast (2 to 2¼ pounds, or 1 kg)

Preheat the oven to 350°F (180°C, or gas mark 4). Coat
a 13 x 9-inch (32.5 x 22.5-cm) baking pan with vegetable
oil spray.

In the pan, combine the peppers, onion, pineapple, sauce,
water, sugar, ginger, and pepper sauce. Stir to mix. Place the
roast in the center of the pan. Spoon some of the mixture
over the roast. Cover loosely with a tent of aluminum foil.

Bake until an instant-read thermometer inserted into the
center registers 155°F (70°C), about 1 hour and 15 minutes.

Prep = 5 minutes **Cook** = 1 hour 15 minutes
Yield = 4 to 6 servings

Alfredo Braised Pork Shoulder

Marcella Hazan, the godmother of Italian cooking, made the original version of this dish popular in America. It's essentially a rich cut of pork simmered gently (braised) in milk. In this version, Alfredo sauce enriches the braising liquid.

1	boneless pork shoulder roast (Boston butt), 2 to 2½ pounds (1 to 1.1 kg)
	Salt and ground black pepper
2	tablespoons (28 ml) olive oil
2	tablespoons (20 g) preminced oil-packed garlic
2 to 3	sprigs fresh marjoram or thyme or 1 teaspoon dried
2½ to 3	cups (590 to 705 ml) milk
1	cup (250 g) refrigerated or jarred Alfredo sauce

Pat dry the roast with paper towels and season all over with salt and pepper. Heat the oil over medium-high heat in a heavy pot just big enough to hold the roast. Add the roast and brown all over, about 10 minutes. Add the garlic and marjoram or thyme and cook for 30 seconds. Gradually add enough milk to come about halfway up the roast (about 1 cup, or 235 ml) and bring to a boil. Reduce the heat to low, cover partially, and simmer gently for about 1 hour, turning the roast now and then. When the milk has thickened into clumps and turned golden brown, stir in additional milk to come about halfway up the roast. Cover and cook until the pork is fork tender, 1½ to 2 hours. Turn the meat now and then, and add milk as necessary to keep the pot from going dry.

Remove the roast to a platter and cover to keep warm. Remove and discard the herb sprigs (if using fresh herbs). Spoon off most of the fat from the pot. Boil over high heat for 2 minutes, scraping the pan bottom. Reduce the heat to low, whisk in the Alfredo sauce, and heat through.

Slice and serve with sauce spooned over top.

Prep = 2 minutes **Cook** = 2½ to 3 hours (mostly unattended)
Yield = 4 to 6 servings

Pork Rollatine with Raisins and Pine Nuts

Thin pieces of stuffed and rolled meat are known as "rollatine" or "braciole" in Italian. Here's a rollatine made with pounded pork loin that was inspired by a recipe in Tony May's terrific primer on Italian cooking, called simply *Italian Cuisine*. If you don't have vodka sauce, use traditional tomato basil sauce instead.

1 pound (455 g) boneless pork loin, sliced ½-inch thick
¼ cup (25 g) grated Asiago or Parmesan cheese
2 tablespoons (20 g) raisins
2 tablespoons (16 g) pine nuts
1 tablespoon (8.6 g) drained small capers
1 tablespoon (10 g) preminced oil-packed garlic
1 tablespoon (7 g) paprika
2 tablespoons (28 ml) olive oil
½ cup (120 ml) sherry
1½ cups (375 g) refrigerated or jarred tomato vodka sauce
1 tablespoon (2.5 g) chopped fresh basil

Prep = 25 minutes   **Cook** = 30 minutes
Yield = 4 to 6 servings

Sprinkle the pork slices with a little water and put between sheets of plastic wrap. Pound with the flat side of a meat mallet or heavy skillet to an even ¼-inch thickness.

Mix 2 tablespoons (10 g) of the cheese with the raisins, pine nuts, capers, and garlic. Divide the filling evenly among the pork slices and roll up. Coat the rolls all over with the paprika. Secure each roll with toothpicks in two places.

Heat the oil in a very large skillet over medium-high heat. Add the rolls and brown all over, 8 to 10 minutes total. Add the sherry and simmer, scraping the pan bottom, until the liquid reduces in volume by about a third. Reduce the heat to medium-low and add the sauce. Spoon some sauce over the rolls, cover the pan, and simmer gently until the pork is no longer pink, 20 to 25 minutes.

Remove the rolls to a platter or plates and allow to rest for 5 minutes. Remove and discard the string and cut the rolls into ½-inch-thick slices. Return any juices from the platter or plates to the pan. Reheat the sauce and serve with the pork. Garnish with the basil and remaining 2 tablespoons (10 g) cheese.

Braised Spareribs with Three Chiles

Grilled pork ribs are great, but those simmered gently in liquid are more forgiving. You're sure to serve up tender, succulent ribs with this method. The heat level here is spicy, but if you prefer it full-on fiery, increase the amount of chipotle. Polenta makes the perfect side dish.

About 3 ½	pounds (1.5 kg) spareribs
2	teaspoons paprika (preferably smoked)
2	teaspoons ground ancho chile
1 to 2	teaspoons ground chipotle chile
½	teaspoon sugar
½	teaspoon salt
¼	teaspoon ground black pepper
½	cup (120 ml) dry red wine
1 ½	cups (375 g) refrigerated or jarred tomato marinara sauce with red wine

Cut the spareribs into individual ribs. Cut close to the bone so there is a large strip of meat on the opposite side of each rib. Combine the paprika, ancho, chipotle, sugar, salt, and black pepper. Coat the ribs all over with the spice mixture.

Preheat the oven to 350°F (180°C, or gas mark 4).

Heat a large, deep ovenproof skillet over medium-high heat. When hot, add the ribs and brown all over, 10 to 12 minutes. Remove to a platter.

Pour the wine into the skillet and boil until the liquid reduces by about half, 2 to 3 minutes, scraping the pan bottom. Reduce the heat to medium and pour in the sauce. Bring to a simmer, then return the ribs to the pan, spooning the sauce over them.

Cover the pan and bake until the rib meat is very tender and pulls away easily from the bones, about 1 hour.

Prep = 5 minutes   **Cook** = 1 hour 15 minutes (mostly unattended)
Yield = 4 servings

Lamb Main Dishes

French Lamb and White Bean Ragout

Slow cooking is the flavor secret of many a French grand-mère. This stew cooks in the oven, but if you prefer a Crock-pot, let it cook for 7 to 8 hours on the low-heat setting. A salad of curly endive, ripe pear slices, and walnuts makes a wonderful accompaniment.

2   pounds (1 kg) well-trimmed lamb stew meat
1   can (15 ounces, or 420 g) great northern or cannellini beans, drained and rinsed
2   cups (8 ounces, or 225 g) frozen pearl onions
¼   cup (30 g) all-purpose flour
¼   cup (15 g) chopped fresh parsley
1   tablespoon (10 g) preminced oil-packed garlic
1   teaspoon herbes de Provence
1   teaspoon ground black pepper
1   cup (250 g) refrigerated or jarred tomato sauce with red wine
½   cup (120 ml) dry red wine

Preheat the oven to 350°F (180°, or gas mark 4). In a large ovenproof pot, combine the lamb, beans, onions, flour, parsley, garlic, herbes, and pepper. Stir until the flour coats all the ingredients. Add the sauce and wine. Stir to mix. Cover tightly. Bake until the lamb is fork tender, about 2 hours.

Prep = 5 minutes   **Cook** = 2 hours
Yield = 4 to 6 servings

North African Lamb Patties with Tomato Mint Sauce

Fresh mint really enlivens the pan sauce for these lamb patties. In a pinch, 1 teaspoon dried mint mixed with 2 tablespoons (8 g) fresh parsley can be used as a replacement. Tuck the patties into warmed pita halves garnished with a dollop of plain yogurt.

- 1½ pounds (680 g) lean ground lamb
- 1½ teaspoons ground cumin
- 1 teaspoon preminced oil-packed garlic
- ½ teaspoon ground black pepper
- ¼ teaspoon salt
- 1 tablespoon (14 ml) olive oil
- 1 cup (250 g) refrigerated or jarred marinara tomato sauce
- 3 tablespoons (18 g) chopped fresh mint leaves

In a bowl, combine the lamb, cumin, garlic, pepper, and salt. Shape into 6 oval patties, about ½-inch thick.

Heat the oil in a large skillet over medium-high heat. Fry the patties, flipping once, until browned on both sides, about 4 minutes total. Remove from heat and spoon off and discard the excess fat in the pan. Return the pan to medium heat. Add the sauce and mint. Cover partially. Reduce the heat so the mixture just simmers. Cook until the patties are no longer pink in the center, about 12 minutes.

Prep = 3 minutes **Cook** = 16 minutes **Yield** = 4 to 6 servings

Shepherd's Pie

This classic British meat-and-potatoes dish is rustic and satisfying. It's cooked and served in the same ovenproof skillet, but, if you prefer, you can transfer the mixture to a shallow 2½-quart (2.5-L) baking dish.

1   recipe Creamy Mashed Potatoes (page 214)
2   tablespoons (28 ml) olive oil
1½   cups (195 g) prechopped onion
½   cup (65 g) prechopped carrots
1   tablespoon (10 g) preminced oil-packed garlic
1½   teaspoons dried thyme
1½   pounds (680 g) ground lamb
1½   cups (375 g) refrigerated or jarred tomato sauce with garlic and onion
½   cup (120 ml) low-sodium chicken broth
¼   teaspoon paprika

Prepare the mashed potatoes according to the recipe directions. Keep warm.

Meanwhile, heat the oil over medium-high heat in a large ovenproof skillet (such as a 10 to 12-inch, or 25 to 30-cm, cast-iron skillet). Add the onions and carrots and cook until the onions are golden, about 5 minutes. Add the garlic, thyme, and lamb and cook, breaking up the meat, just until it is no longer pink, 4 to 6 minutes. Stir in the tomato sauce and broth. Reduce the heat to medium-low and continue cooking until very thick, 20 to 25 minutes.

Preheat the broiler. Spread the mashed potatoes over the meat. Drag the tines of a fork through the top of the potatoes to create wavy lines on the surface. Sprinkle with the paprika and broil about 4 inches (10 cm) from the heat until lightly browned, 2 to 3 minutes.

Prep = 5 minutes   **Cook** = 35 minutes   **Yield** = 6 servings

Moussaka

Greeks know lamb and this casserole is a Greek favorite. Layers of savory eggplant are surrounded by seasoned ground lamb and white sauce flavored with mint, allspice, and feta cheese. This version uses both tomato and Alfredo sauces from your pantry.

3 tablespoons (42 ml) olive oil

2 cups (260 g) prechopped onion

1 teaspoon preminced oil-packed garlic

1¾ pounds (795 g) ground lamb

1 tablespoon fresh chopped mint or
   1½ teaspoons dried mint or oregano

1 teaspoon ground allspice

1 teaspoon ground black pepper

1 teaspoon salt

1½ cups (375 g) refrigerated or jarred
   marinara tomato sauce

2 large eggplants (2 to 2½ pounds, or 1 to 1.1 kg)

1 large egg

1½ cups (375 g) refrigerated or jarred Alfredo sauce

¾ cup (2 ounces, or 55 g) crumbled feta cheese

Prep = 15 minutes   **Cook** = 55 minutes (mostly unattended)
Yield = 6 to 8 servings

Heat 1 tablespoon (14 ml) of the oil in a large skillet over medium heat. Add the onion and cook until golden, about 5 minutes. Increase the heat to high and add the garlic, lamb, mint or oregano, allspice, ½ teaspoon pepper, and ½ teaspoon salt. Cook, breaking up the meat, just until it is no longer pink, 4 to 6 minutes. Stir in the tomato sauce, reduce the heat to medium-low, and simmer gently until slightly thickened, 15 to 20 minutes.

Meanwhile, preheat the broiler. Peel the eggplants and slice them lengthwise into slabs about ⅜-inch thick. Put the slabs on a large baking sheet and brush both sides with the remaining 2 tablespoons (28 ml) olive oil. Sprinkle with the remaining ½ teaspoon salt and ½ teaspoon pepper. Broil 4 to 5 inches (10 to 13 cm) from the heat until lightly browned, 3 to 5 minutes per side.

In a medium bowl, beat together the egg, Alfredo, and feta.

Reduce the oven temperature to 350ºF (180ºC, or gas mark 4). Arrange a layer of eggplant in the bottom of a shallow 2½-quart (2.5-L) baking dish (such as an 11 x 7-inch, or 27.5 x 17.5-cm, dish). Spoon a layer of the lamb mixture over top. Add another layer of eggplant, another layer of lamb, and a final layer of eggplant. Poke in several places with a fork. Pour the Alfredo mixture over top.

Bake until set and golden brown on top, 30 to 35 minutes. Let stand 15 minutes before cutting.

Creamy
Lamb Curry

Made with almond butter and
creamy tomato sauce, this curry is
decadently rich. Add some frozen peas
if you like. Look for almond butter in
the natural foods section of your store or
near the peanut butter. If you can't find it, grind
½ cup (65 g) blanched almonds in a food processor
along with the vodka tomato sauce. Garnish with
sliced almonds and chopped fresh cilantro.

1½ pounds (680 g) boneless leg of lamb,
    cut into 1-inch (2.5-cm) cubes
 1 tablespoon (10 g) Madras curry powder
 ½ teaspoon salt
    Pinch of cayenne pepper or more to taste
 1 tablespoon (14 ml) vegetable oil
 2 cups (260 g) prechopped onion
 1 tablespoon (10 g) preminced oil-packed garlic
 2 teaspoons jarred pregrated fresh ginger
 2 cups (500 g) refrigerated or jarred vodka tomato sauce
 ½ cup (130 g) almond butter
 1 cup (480 ml) heavy cream or half-and-half

Coat the lamb all over with the curry powder, salt, and
cayenne pepper.

Heat the oil in a medium saucepan or deep, wide skillet
over medium-high heat. Add the lamb and brown all over,
stirring now and then, about 5 minutes. Remove to a platter.

Add the onions to the pan and cook until golden, about 4
minutes. Add the garlic and ginger and cook 1 minute.
Reduce the heat to medium-low and add the tomato sauce,
almond butter, and cream, stirring thoroughly. Return the
lamb and its juices to the pan, cover, and simmer gently until
the lamb is tender, 25 to 30 minutes.

Prep = 5 minutes   **Cook** = 35 minutes
Yield = 4 servings

Grilled Lamb
with Pesto

Here's a dish with big rewards for very
little work. Just marinate a butterflied
leg of lamb in doctored-up pesto, then
grill it for 30 minutes. Risotto or couscous
makes a perfect side dish.

- 2 lemons
- ½ cup (120 g) refrigerated or jarred basil pesto
- 2 tablespoons (28 ml) extra-virgin olive oil
- 1 teaspoon paprika, preferably smoked
- 1 boneless butterflied leg of lamb (3½ to 4 pounds, or 1.5 to 1.8 kg)

Grate the zest from both lemons into a bowl. Squeeze the
juice from one of the lemons into the bowl. Stir in the pesto,
olive oil, and paprika. Rub all over the lamb, cover, and refrigerate at least 8 hours or overnight.

Bring the lamb to room temperature, about 20 minutes.

Preheat the grill to medium-high. Grill the lamb directly
over the heat, turning often, until a thermometer inserted
in the center registers 130°F (55°C) for medium-rare, about
30 to 35 minutes. Let rest for 10 minutes before slicing.

Cut the remaining lemons into wedges and pass at the
table for squeezing.

Prep = 5 minutes + 8 hours marinating **Cook** = 30 minutes
Yield = 10 to 12 servings

Moroccan Lamb
with Couscous

Don't be put off by the lengthy ingredients list here. It's mostly spices that are mixed together and tossed with lamb. Prep time here is only 5 minutes and the entire meal comes together in less than 30 minutes.

1	box (6 ounces, or 170 g) couscous with toasted pine nuts
½	teaspoon ground coriander
½	teaspoon ground cumin
¼	teaspoon crushed saffron threads or ground turmeric
¼	teaspoon ground cinnamon
¼	teaspoon ground black pepper
¼	teaspoon salt
	Pinch of cayenne pepper or more to taste
1¼	pounds (570 g) boneless leg of lamb, cut into 1-inch (2.5-cm) cubes
2	tablespoons (28 ml) olive oil
1½	cups (195 g) prechopped onion
1	tablespoon (10 g) preminced oil-packed garlic
2	teaspoons jarred pregrated fresh ginger
½	cup (75 g) raisins
2	cups (500 g) refrigerated or jarred tomato sauce with garlic and onion

Prep = 5 minutes   **Cook** = 20 minutes   **Yield** = 4 servings

Prepare the couscous according to the package directions. Meanwhile, combine the coriander, cumin, saffron or turmeric, cinnamon, black pepper, salt, and cayenne pepper in a medium bowl. Toss with the lamb cubes to coat evenly.

Heat the oil in a medium saucepan over medium-high heat. Add the lamb and cook until browned all over, about 5 minutes, stirring now and then. Remove to a platter and cover to keep warm.

Reduce the heat to medium, add the onions, and cook until golden, about 4 minutes. Add the garlic and ginger and cook for 1 minute. Add the raisins, tomato sauce, and ½ cup (120 ml) water. Bring to a simmer, then reduce the heat to medium-low and return the lamb to the pan. Simmer gently until the flavors have blended, 10 to 12 minutes.

Serve the lamb alongside the couscous.

Provençal Braised Lamb Shanks

   2   teaspoons paprika
  ½   teaspoon crushed dried rosemary or thyme
  ¼   teaspoon salt
  ¼   teaspoon ground black pepper
   4   lamb shanks (3 to 3½ pounds, or 1.4 to 1.6 kg , total)
  ¾   cup (90 g) all-purpose flour
   1   tablespoon (14 ml) olive oil
   2   cups (260 g) prechopped onion
   2   tablespoons (20 g) preminced oil-packed garlic
   1   bay leaf
   1   cup (235 ml) dry white wine
   1   cup (235 ml) low-sodium chicken broth
  1½ cups (375 g) refrigerated or jarred tomato
       marinara sauce
       Zest and juice of 1 lemon
  ⅓   cup (30 g) pitted and halved oil-cured black olives

Preheat the oven to 325ºF (170°C, or gas mark 3).
Combine the paprika, rosemary or thyme, salt, and black
pepper. Coat the lamb shanks all over with the spice mixture.
Dredge the lamb in the flour (or sprinkle the flour all over
the lamb) and pat off any excess.

Heat the oil over medium heat in a Dutch oven or other
large ovenproof pot. Add the lamb shanks (in batches, if necessary, to avoid crowding) and brown all over, 8 to 10 minutes. Remove to a plate.

Discard all but 1 tablespoon (14 ml) fat from the pan. Add
the onions and cook until golden, about 4 minutes. Add the
garlic and bay leaf and cook 1 minute. Add the wine and simmer, scraping the pan bottom, until the liquid is reduced by
about half. Add the broth, sauce, and lemon zest (reserve the
lemon juice) and bring to a simmer. Return the lamb shanks
to the pot and spoon some sauce over them. Cover and bake
in the oven until the meat is fork tender, about 2 hours.

Remove and discard the bay leaf and spoon off excess fat
from the surface of the sauce. Stir in the lemon juice and
olives. Serve the shanks with the sauce.

Prep = 5 minutes   **Cook** = 2 to 2½ hours
(mostly unattended)   **Yield** = 4 servings

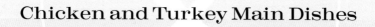

Chicken and Turkey Main Dishes

Chicken Scaloppine with Creamy Mushroom Sauce

Available prepackaged in supermarkets, ultrathin cutlets of chicken cook in less than 5 minutes. You could use turkey, veal, or pork cutlets instead.

3   tablespoons (42 g) butter, divided
1½ pounds (680 g) presliced chicken scaloppine
8   ounces (225 g) presliced brown mushrooms
½   teaspoon ground black pepper
⅛   teaspoon ground nutmeg
    Salt
1   cup (250 g) refrigerated or jarred Alfredo sauce
2   tablespoons (8 g) minced fresh parsley (optional)

In a large skillet, heat 1 tablespoon (14 g) butter over medium-high heat. Add half of the scaloppine. Cook until browned, about 2 minutes per side. Remove to a plate. Repeat with 1 tablespoon (14 g) of butter and the remaining scaloppine. Remove to a plate.

Add the remaining 1 tablespoon (14 g) butter, mushrooms, pepper, nutmeg, and a pinch of salt to the pan. Toss. Cover and cook, tossing occasionally, over medium heat, until the mushrooms give off their liquid, about 5 minutes. Uncover and cook until most of the liquid evaporates. Reduce the heat to medium-low. Stir in the Alfredo sauce. Return the scaloppine, plus any juices accumulated on the plate, to the pan. Simmer until heated through, about 2 minutes. Sprinkle with parsley, if using.

Prep = 3 minutes   **Cook** = 12 minutes   **Yield** = 4 to 6 servings

Chicken Parmigiana

Prepared sauce and presliced chicken scaloppine make this classic dish simple to prepare.

½ cup (60 g) all-purpose flour
1 large egg, lightly beaten
1 cup (115 g) seasoned dry bread crumbs
¾ cup (75 g) grated Parmesan cheese
2 tablespoons (8 g) chopped fresh parsley
1½ pounds (680 g) presliced chicken scaloppine
¼ cup (60 ml) olive oil
1¾ cups (430 g) refrigerated or jarred traditional tomato basil sauce
6 ounces (170 g) mozzarella cheese, thinly sliced

Put the flour in one shallow bowl and the egg in another. Mix the bread crumbs, ¼ cup (25 g) of the Parmesan, and 1 tablespoon (4 g) of the parsley in a third shallow bowl. Coat the chicken with the flour and shake off the excess. Roll in the egg, then coat evenly with the bread crumbs. Repeat with the remaining chicken.

Heat the oil in a large heavy skillet over medium-high heat. Add the chicken and cook until golden brown on both sides, 2 to 3 minutes per side.

Preheat the oven to 350°F (180°C, or gas mark 4).

Pour 1 tablespoon (14 g) of the oil from the skillet into a 13 x 9-inch (32.5 x 22.5-cm) baking dish. Pour in ½ cup (125 g) of the tomato sauce and spread evenly. Arrange the chicken over the sauce, overlapping the pieces as necessary. Pour the remaining 1¼ cups (315 g) sauce over the chicken. Arrange the mozzarella slices over the chicken and scatter on the remaining ½ cup (50 g) Parmesan.

Cover with foil and bake until hot and bubbly, 20 to 25 minutes. To brown the cheese, uncover and turn on the broiler. Broil about 4 inches (10 cm) from the heat until lightly browned, 1 to 3 minutes. Sprinkle with the remaining 1 tablespoon (4 g) chopped fresh parsley.

Prep = 15 minutes   **Cook** = 30 minutes   **Yield** = 4 servings

Pan-Seared Chicken with Eggplant Sauce

For a meatier-tasting dish, brown 8 ounces loose Italian sausage in the skillet after searing the chicken. Serve this 30-minute meal with rice or noodles.

1½ pounds (680 g) boneless, skinless chicken breasts or thighs
   Salt and ground black pepper
1 teaspoon paprika
   All-purpose flour
3 tablespoons (42 ml) olive oil
1 medium eggplant (about 12 ounces, or 340 g), unpeeled, cut into bite-size pieces
1 tablespoon (10 g) preminced oil-packed garlic
½ teaspoon fennel seed
1 jar (26 ounces, or 737 g) tomato marinara sauce with red wine
¾ cup (175 ml) low-sodium chicken broth
2 teaspoons chopped fresh rosemary

Preheat oven to 350ºF (180ºC, or gas mark 4).
   Lightly season the chicken all over with salt and pepper and the paprika. Roll in flour, patting off the excess.
   Heat 2 tablespoons (28 ml) of the oil in a large ovenproof skillet over medium-high heat. Add the chicken and brown all over, 4 to 5 minutes. Remove to a platter and keep warm.
   Add the remaining 1 tablespoon (14 ml) oil to the skillet. Lightly season the eggplant with salt and pepper and add to the skillet. Cook, stirring frequently, for 2 to 3 minutes. Add the garlic and fennel seed and cook for 1 minute. Stir in the sauce, broth, and rosemary. Remove from the heat and return the chicken to the pan, spooning some sauce over top. Cover and bake until the chicken is no longer pink in the center (165ºF, or 75ºC, on an instant-read thermometer), about 15 minutes.

Prep = 5 minutes   **Cook** = 25 minutes   **Yield** = 4 servings

North Indian Chicken in Warmly Spiced Tomato Sauce

The Indian spice mixture garam masala is becoming increasingly available in supermarkets. It's typically a combination of black pepper, cinnamon, cloves, coriander, cumin, cardamom, dried chiles, fennel, mace, and nutmeg. If you like, curry powder can replace the garam masala for a different flavoring.

- 2 tablespoons (28 ml) vegetable oil
- 1½ pounds (680 g) boneless, skinless chicken breasts or thighs, cut into bite-size chunks
- 1 cup (4 ounces, or 115 g) prechopped tricolored bell peppers
- 2 bunches scallions, all parts, cut into 1-inch (2.5-cm) pieces (1½ cups, or 150 g)
- 1 serrano chile, minced
- 1 tablespoon (10 g) preminced oil-packed garlic
- 2 teaspoons refrigerated pregrated fresh ginger
- 2 teaspoons ground garam masala
- 1 cup (250 g) refrigerated or jarred tomato marinara sauce
- ¼ cup (60 ml) water

Heat the oil in a large skillet set over medium-high heat. Add the chicken. Toss until no pink is visible, about 5 minutes. Add the bell peppers, scallions, chile, garlic, ginger, and garam masala. Increase the heat to high. Cook, tossing, until a golden crust forms on the bottom of the pan, about 4 minutes. Add the sauce and water. Scrape the pan bottom to release browned bits. Reduce the heat to medium-low. Cook at a slow simmer until the chicken is cooked through, about 3 minutes.

Prep = 3 minutes   **Cook** = 12 minutes
Yield = 4 to 6 servings

Jamaican Chicken Curry

Here's a simplified version of Jamaican goat curry, one of the island's most popular dishes. Serve it with rice and jarred mango chutney.

2	tablespoons (18 g) curry powder
2	Scotch bonnet, habanero, or jalapeño chiles, seeded and minced
1	tablespoon (10 g) preminced oil-packed garlic
1	large scallion, finely chopped
½	teaspoon salt
¼	teaspoon ground black pepper
¼	cup (60 ml) vegetable oil
2	pounds (1 kg) boneless, skinless chicken thighs, cut into 1-inch (2.5-cm) pieces
2	cups (260 g) prechopped onion
1½	cups (375 g) refrigerated or jarred tomato sauce with garlic and onion
1 to 1½	cups (235 to 355 ml) low-sodium chicken broth or water

In a large bowl, combine the curry powder, chiles, garlic, scallion, salt, pepper, and 2 tablespoons (28 ml) of the oil. Add the chicken and toss to coat completely. Cover and refrigerate for at least 2 hours or up to 12 hours.

When ready to cook, let the chicken rest at room temperature for 30 minutes. Heat the remaining 2 tablespoons (28 ml) oil in a Dutch oven or large, deep skillet over medium-high heat. Remove the chicken from the marinade, reserving the marinade. Add the chicken to the pan (in batches, if necessary, to prevent crowding) and brown all over, 5 to 7 minutes. Remove to a plate and keep warm. Add onions to the pan and cook until golden, about 4 minutes. Add the sauce, broth, and reserved marinade, and bring to a boil. Reduce the heat to low, and return the chicken to the pan. Cover and simmer very gently until the meat is tender and the sauce has thickened like gravy, 30 to 40 minutes.

Prep = 5 minutes + 2 to 12 hours for marinating
Cook = 1¼ hours (mostly unattended)   **Yield** = 4 servings

Buffalo Chicken Casserole

Why use buffalo sauce for chicken wings alone? Here, the zesty sauce flavors a soon-to-be-popular main dish.

3	tablespoons (42 ml) olive oil
2 to 2¼	pounds (1 kg) boneless, skinless chicken thighs
	All-purpose flour
¾	cup (120 g) prechopped celery
¾	cup (98 g) prechopped onion
1	cup (250 g) refrigerated or jarred tomato sauce with garlic and onion
1	tablespoon (16 g) mild hot pepper sauce, such as Frank's or Crystal
¾	cup (90 g) precrumbled blue cheese

Preheat the oven to 350°F (180°C, or gas mark 4). Coat a 13 x 9-inch (32.5 x 22.5-cm) baking dish with vegetable oil spray.

Heat the oil in a large skillet set over high heat. Dust the chicken with flour, shaking off excess. Place in the pan and fry until golden on both sides, about 5 minutes total. Transfer to the prepared baking dish. Reduce the heat to medium. Add the celery and onion to the pan, scraping the pan bottom to remove the browned bits. Cook, stirring, until golden, about 2 minutes. Add the tomato sauce and hot pepper sauce. Bring almost to a boil. Pour over the reserved chicken. Cover the baking dish with aluminum foil.

Bake for 20 minutes. Remove the foil. Scatter the cheese over the chicken. Bake until the cheese bubbles, about 10 minutes.

Prep = 5 minutes   **Cook** = 37 minutes
Yield = 4 to 6 servings

Easy Chicken Pot Pie

Rotisserie chickens are the quick cook's lifesaver. For this creamy pot pie, use a small rotisserie chicken, discard the skin and bones, and cut the meat into chunks (about 2½ cups meat).

2	tablespoons (28 ml) vegetable oil
1½	cups (195 g) prechopped onion
1½	cups (195 g) prechopped carrots
1	cup (160 g) prechopped celery
2	tablespoons (15 g) all-purpose flour
1½	cups (355 ml) low-sodium chicken broth
2	cups (500 g) refrigerated or jarred Alfredo sauce
1¼	pounds (570 g) cooked chicken, cut into bite-size chunks
¾	cup (98 g) frozen peas
2	tablespoons (8 g) chopped fresh parsley
1	recipe Parmesan Cream Biscuits (page 212) unbaked or 1 pound (455 g) prepared biscuit dough

Preheat oven to 400 °F (200 °C, or gas mark 6). Heat the oil in a large skillet over medium-high heat. Add the onions, carrots, and celery and cook until the vegetables are just tender, 5 to 7 minutes. Stir in the flour and cook 1 minute. Whisk in the broth and cook until slightly thickened, about 3 minutes. Remove from the heat and stir in the Alfredo sauce, chicken, peas, and parsley.

Scrape the chicken filling into a 13 x 9-inch (32.5 x 22.5-cm) baking dish. Arrange the cut-out biscuit dough over the filling and bake until bubbly and the biscuits are lightly browned on top, 20 to 25 minutes.

Prep = 2 minutes   **Cook** = 30 minutes
Yield = 6 servings

Chicken Paprikash

Look for sweet Hungarian paprika
sold in tins in the supermarket spice aisle.
If you like, a little hot paprika will give the dish
a dash of attitude. Serve with buttered noodles
tossed with chopped fresh dill or parsley.

1½   pounds (680 g) boneless, skin-on chicken thighs
 2   tablespoons (14 g) paprika
    Salt and ground black pepper
 2   tablespoons (28 g) butter
1½   cups (195 g) prechopped onion
 2   teaspoons preminced oil-packed garlic
1½   cups (375 g) refrigerated or jarred tomato sauce
    with garlic and onion
 ½   cup (120 ml) chicken broth
 ½   cup (120 g) sour cream

Toss the chicken with 1 tablespoon (7 g) of the paprika and
season lightly with salt and pepper.

Heat 1 tablespoon (14 g) of the butter in a large skillet over
medium-high heat. Add the chicken (in batches, if necessary,
to prevent crowding) and brown all over, 5 minutes. Remove
to a plate and cover with foil to keep warm.

Melt the remaining 1 tablespoon (14 g) butter in the skillet,
add the onions, and cook until golden, 3 to 4 minutes. Add
the garlic and remaining 1 tablespoon paprika (7 g) and cook
1 minute. Add the tomato sauce and broth. Reduce the heat
to medium and simmer until slightly thickened, 5 to 8 minutes. Stir in the sour cream, then return the chicken to the
pan and cook until the chicken is no longer pink in the center
(about 165°F, or 75°C, on an instant-read thermometer),
about 5 minutes.

Prep = 2 minutes   **Cook** = 20 minutes
Yield = 4 servings

Chicken Thighs in Hunter Sauce

Hunter sauce or "cacciatore" is a perennial Italian favorite because the ingredients are readily at hand. Like most of the dishes in this book, this cacciatore requires no chopping. Serve it with cooked rice and garnish with chopped fresh basil.

3	pounds (1.4 kg) bone-in, skin-in chicken thighs
	Salt and ground black pepper
2	tablespoons (28 ml) olive oil
1	cup (130 g) prechopped onion
1½	cups (195 g) prechopped bell peppers
8	ounces (225 g) presliced mushrooms
1	tablespoon (10 g) preminced oil-packed garlic
½	teaspoon dried rosemary
½	teaspoon fennel seeds
¼	teaspoon crushed red pepper flakes
2½	cups (750 g) refrigerated or jarred marinara tomato sauce with red wine

Lightly season the chicken with salt and black pepper. Heat the oil in a large, deep skillet over medium-high heat. Add the chicken (in batches, if necessary, to prevent crowding) and brown all over, 6 to 8 minutes. Remove to a plate.

Add the onions and cook until softened, 3 to 4 minutes. Add the bell peppers and cook until just softened, 3 to 4 minutes. Add the mushrooms, garlic, rosemary, fennel, and red pepper flakes. Cook for 2 minutes. Add the sauce and return the chicken to the pan, spooning some sauce over top. Reduce the heat to low, cover, and cook until the chicken juices run clear when pierced, 10 to 15 minutes. Uncover and cook over medium-high heat until slightly thickened, 2 to 4 minutes.

Prep = 2 minutes   **Cook** = 35 minutes
Yield = 4 servings

Braised Chicken with Spinach

Prep time is minimal here and the Alfredo sauce and spinach enrich the braising liquid to serve as a sauce. Risotto makes the perfect side dish.

3½ to 4   pounds (1.6 to 1.8 kg) chicken parts
          Salt and ground black pepper
      2   tablespoons (28 ml) olive oil
      2   tablespoons (20 g) preminced oil-packed garlic
1 to 1½   cups (235 to 355 ml) milk
      1   bay leaf
   3 to 4 leaves fresh sage or ½ teaspoon dried
      2   cups (3 to 4 ounces, or 85 to 115 g) prewashed baby spinach leaves
      1   cup (250 g) refrigerated or jarred Alfredo sauce

Pat dry the chicken with paper towels and season lightly with salt and pepper. Heat the oil in a deep, wide skillet over medium-high heat. Add the chicken and brown all over, about 5 minutes. Add the garlic and cook for 30 seconds. Gradually add enough milk to barely cover the chicken (about 1 cup, or 235 ml) and bring to a boil, scraping the pan bottom. Add the bay leaf and sage and reduce the heat to medium-low. Cover partially and simmer gently until the chicken juices run clear when pricked with a knife, 25 to 30 minutes, turning the chicken pieces now and then. Add additional milk if necessary to keep the chicken partially covered.

Remove the chicken to a platter and cover to keep warm. Bring the braising liquid to a boil over high heat and boil until reduced in volume by about half. Reduce the heat to medium-low and remove and discard the bay leaf and sage (if using fresh sage). Stir in the spinach and Alfredo sauce and cook until heated through and the spinach begins to wilt, 2 to 3 minutes.

Serve the chicken with the sauce spooned over top.

Prep = 2 minutes   **Cook** = 40 minutes (mostly unattended)
Yield = 4 to 6 servings

Chicken and Avocado Salad with Creamy Sun-Dried Tomato Dressing

If you have leftover Lemon Basil Roast Chicken (page 98), enjoy it again in this salad. Or, use a small rotisserie chicken, remove and discard the skin and bones, and cut the meat into bite-size chunks (about 2½ cups).

- 1 cup (250 g) refrigerated or jarred sun-dried tomato Alfredo sauce
- 1½ teaspoons dried cumin
- 1¼ pounds (570 g) cooked chicken, cut into bite-size chunks
- 1 bunch sliced scallions, white and light green parts (⅓ cup, or 30 g)
- 6 cups (6 ounces, or 170 g) spring salad mix
- 1 avocado, cubed
- 1 cup (4 ounces, or 115 g) grape tomatoes, halved

In a large bowl, combine the sauce and cumin. Add the chicken and scallions, stirring gently. Place the spring mix on 6 dinner plates. Top with the chicken salad and garnish with the avocado and tomato.

Prep = 5 minutes   **Yield** = 4 to 6 servings

Lemon Basil Roast Chicken

1 whole chicken (about 4 pounds, or 1.8 kg), giblets removed
1 small lemon
½ cup (130 g) refrigerated or jarred basil pesto
Salt and ground black pepper
¼ cup (56 g) butter, melted

Preheat the oven to 400°F (200°C, or gas mark 6).

Trim the chicken of excess fat, then rinse inside and out. Pat dry with paper towels, then loosen the skin all over the chicken (it might not loosen in some spots, which is okay).

Grate the lemon zest into a bowl, then stir in the pesto. Using your fingers or a small rubber spatula, spread most of the pesto mixture between the skin and meat of the chicken, especially over the breast, thighs, and drumsticks. Spread the remaining mixture inside the chicken cavity. Cut the zested lemon into quarters and put them in the chicken cavity.

Place the chicken on a V-rack or flat roasting rack in a shallow roasting pan. Season the outside of the chicken all over with salt and pepper and brush with some of the melted butter. Put the chicken on its side on the rack (the leg should be facing up). If using a flat rack, steady the chicken by putting balls of aluminum foil beneath it.

Roast in the oven for 20 to 25 minutes. Brush with additional butter, then invert the chicken so the other leg is facing up (grab the bird with heatproof gloves or insert a wooden spoon into the cavity). Steady the chicken as necessary, then roast for another 20 to 25 minutes. Brush with more butter, then turn the bird breast-side up and brush with the remaining butter. Roast until an instant-read thermometer inserted into the thickest part of a thigh registers 165°F (75°C), 15 to 20 minutes more.

Tilt the bird upright so that its juices flow into the pan.

Prep = 20 minutes   **Cook** = About 1 hour (mostly unattended)   **Yield** = 4 servings

Turkey Tetrazzini

Opera singer Luisa Tetrazzini was famous
in the early 1900s for her beautiful soprano voice,
as well as for her appetite. This rich and creamy
dish combines her favorite foods: poultry,
mushrooms, and noodles.

- 8   ounces (225 g) egg noodles or spaghetti
- 1½ pounds (680 g) turkey breast cutlets
- 2   cups (470 ml) chicken broth
- 2   tablespoons (28 g) butter
- 8   ounces (225 g) presliced cremini or white mushrooms
- 3   tablespoons (42 ml) dry sherry
- 1½ cups (375 g) refrigerated or jarred Alfredo sauce
- ½   cup (50 g) grated Parmesan cheese

Cook the noodles according to the package directions. Butter
a 13 x 9-inch (32.5 x 22.5-cm) baking dish.

Meanwhile, put the turkey and broth in a Dutch oven or a
large, deep skillet. Bring to a boil over high heat, then reduce
the heat to medium-low, cover, and simmer very gently until the
juices run clear when the turkey is pierced, 8 to 10 minutes.

Remove the turkey to a cutting board and cut into bite-size
pieces. Pour the broth into a 2-cup (470-ml) glass measure.

Preheat the oven to 375°F (190°C, or gas mark 5).

Melt the butter over medium-high heat in the same pan
used to cook the turkey. Add the mushrooms and cook until
they release their liquid, about 5 minutes. Add the sherry and
cook 1 minute. Stir in 1 cup (235 ml) of the reserved broth, the
Alfredo sauce, and the turkey. Remove from the heat.

Drain the pasta and add the turkey mixture, stirring until
combined. Scrape the mixture into the prepared dish and
sprinkle with the Parmesan. Bake until bubbly and lightly
browned on top, 25 to 30 minutes.

Prep = 5 minutes   **Cook** = 40 minutes
Yield = 6 servings

Crispy Cajun Turkey Tenders

Alfredo sauce coats these tantalizing
tenders, adding moisture and flavor.
It also helps the bread crumbs to stick.

1½ to 1¾	pounds (680 to 795 g) turkey tenderloins
1½	cups (375 g) refrigerated or jarred Alfredo sauce
1½	cups (170 g) plain dry bread crumbs
1	tablespoon (7 g) plus 2 teaspoons Cajun seasoning mix
1	cup (250 g) refrigerated or jarred tomato sauce with garlic and onion

Preheat the oven to 400°F (200°C, or gas mark 6). Coat a
large baking sheet with vegetable oil spray.

Cut the tenderloins into ¾-inch wide diagonal strips.
Pour the Alfredo sauce into a pie plate or other shallow container. On a large sheet of waxed paper, placed next to the
sauce, combine the bread crumbs and Cajun seasoning. One
at a time, dip the tenders into the sauce, shaking off excess.
Roll the dipped tenders in the crumbs, shaking off excess.
Transfer to the baking sheet. Repeat with the remaining tenders. Leave at least ½ inch of space between the tenders (if
necessary, use 2 baking sheets).

Bake until browned and the turkey is no longer pink in the
center, about 18 minutes.

Place the tomato sauce in a microwaveable dish. Cover
with waxed paper. Cook in the microwave on high power until
heated through, about 1 minute. Serve with the tenders for
dipping.

Prep = 10 minutes **Cook** = 18 minutes
Yield = 6 servings

Turkey and Broccoli Stir-Sauté in Cheddar Sauce

Make this skillet dish a complete meal by serving it over instant brown rice or noodles. Of course, a salad wouldn't hurt the meal.

- 2 tablespoons (28 ml) vegetable oil, divided
- 4 strips precooked bacon
- 2 bags (8 ounces, or 225 g, each) broccoli florets, cut into bite-size pieces (8 cups)
- ½ cup (2 ounces, or 55 g) prechopped onion
- ¼ cup (60 ml) water
- 1 pound (455 g) boneless skinless turkey breast fillets, cut into bite-size strips
- 1 cup (230 g) refrigerated or jarred cheddar cheese sauce

In a large skillet, heat 1 tablespoon (14 ml) oil over medium-high heat. Add the bacon. Cook, turning, until crisp, about 1 minute. Remove to a paper-towel-lined plate. Add the broccoli and onion. Stir to coat with oil. Cover and cook, stirring occasionally, for 4 minutes, or until the broccoli is starting to brown. Remove to a plate and set aside. Add the water. Scrape to remove browned particles. Pour over the broccoli. Heat the remaining 1 tablespoon (14 ml) oil in the skillet set over medium-high heat. Add the turkey. Cook, stirring frequently, until browned, about 2 minutes. Return the broccoli, onion, and the juices on the plate, to the pan. Add the sauce and stir to mix. Simmer over medium-low heat for 2 minutes, or until the turkey is cooked through. Crumble the bacon and sprinkle on top.

Prep = 5 minutes   **Cook** = 10 minutes
Yield = 4 to 6 servings

Turkey Cutlets in Tomato Caper Sauce

Look for super-thin turkey cutlets in your grocer's meat case. You could use chicken or veal cutlets here. Garnish with chopped fresh basil and grated Parmesan.

1½ pounds (680 g) presliced turkey breast cutlets
    Salt and ground black pepper
 ½ cup (60 g) all-purpose flour
 4 tablespoons (56 g) butter
 ¼ cup (33 g) prechopped onion
 1 tablespoon (10 g) preminced oil-packed garlic
 ¼ teaspoon crushed red pepper flakes
    Pinch of saffron threads, crushed
 ½ cup (120 ml) dry white wine
1½ cups (375 g) refrigerated or jarred tomato basil sauce
 2 tablespoons (17 g) drained capers

Lightly season the turkey cutlets with salt and pepper. Roll in the flour, patting off the excess.

Heat 1½ tablespoons (21 g) of the butter in a large skillet over medium-high heat. Add half of the turkey cutlets. Cook until browned, about 2 minutes per side. Remove to a plate. Repeat with 1½ tablespoons (21 g) of the butter and the remaining turkey cutlets. Remove to a plate.

Add the remaining 1 tablespoon (14 g) butter and onions. Cook until the onions are golden, 3 to 4 minutes. Add the garlic, red pepper flakes, and saffron and cook 1 minute. Stir in the wine, scraping the pan bottom and boil until the liquid is reduced by about half. Stir in the sauce, capers, and any juices from the turkey plate. Reduce the heat to medium-low and simmer gently until heated through, 3 to 4 minutes. Serve the sauce with the turkey.

Prep = 2 minutes   **Cook** = 13 minutes   **Yield** = 4 to 6 servings

Fish and Shellfish Main Dishes

Southern Catfish with Tomato Okra Sauce

Oven-fried fish tastes as good
as good-fried but without the mess. Choose
tiny fresh okra so they stay crisp when cooked.

CATFISH:

- 6 tablespoons (84 g) melted butter, divided
- 1 cup (235 ml) buttermilk or milk
- 1 cup (135 g) cornmeal
- 1 teaspoon paprika
- 2 pounds (1 kg) catfish fillets

TOMATO-OKRA SAUCE:

- 2 tablespoons (28 ml) vegetable oil
- 12 ounces (340 g) small okra, cut into halves or thirds
- 1 cup (130 g) prechopped onion
- 1 cup (250 g) refrigerated or jarred tomato sauce with garlic and onion
- 6 lemon wedges

FOR THE CATFISH: Preheat the oven to 425°F (220°C, or gas mark 7). Drizzle 3 tablespoons (42 g) of butter onto a large baking sheet with sides. Set aside.

Pour the buttermilk or milk into a pie plate or large shallow dish. On a sheet of waxed paper combine the cornmeal and paprika. Toss with a fork to mix. One at a time, dip the catfish fillets into the milk. Remove, shaking off excess. Dip into the cornmeal, patting to adhere. Place on the prepared pan. When all of the fillets are coated, drizzle with the remaining 3 tablespoons (42 g) butter. Bake until the fillets are opaque in the center, about 12 minutes.

FOR THE SAUCE: Meanwhile, heat the oil in a large skillet over medium-high heat. Add the okra and onion. Cover and cook, stirring occasionally, until browned, about 5 minutes. Add the sauce. Bring almost to a boil. Reduce the heat to keep warm. Serve the sauce with the fish. Garnish with lemon wedges.

Prep = 10 minutes **Cook** = 12 minutes **Yield** = 4 to 6 servings

Caribbean Red Snapper with Avocado

Any mild white-fleshed fish, such as tilapia, catfish, or haddock, works well for this light and flavor-filled main dish.

- ¼ cup (60 ml) olive oil
- 1 tablespoon (10 g) preminced oil-packed garlic
- 1 cup (250 g) refrigerated or jarred tomato sauce with garlic and onion
- ¼ cup (60 ml) water
- 1 teaspoon dried thyme
- ½ teaspoon ground cayenne pepper
- 2 to 2 ½ pounds (1 to 1.1 kg) red snapper fillets
- 1 avocado, sliced
- 6 lime wedges

In a large skillet, heat the oil and garlic over low heat until fragrant, about 2 minutes. Add the sauce, water, thyme, and cayenne. Increase the heat to medium and bring to a boil. Place the fish in the pan. Spoon some of the sauce over the fish. Reduce the heat so the sauce simmers moderately. Cover and cook until the fish is just a bit filmy and moist in the center, about 8 minutes. Carefully remove the fish to plates. Add the avocado to the pan and simmer for 1 minute. Spoon over the reserved fish. Garnish with the lime wedges for squeezing.

Prep = 3 minutes **Cook** = 12 minutes
Yield = 4 to 6 servings

Broiled Bass with Bacon, Red Pesto, and Capers

If you can find it, use sea bass for the best flavor. Farmed striped bass tends to have a milder taste. You could also use mahimahi or halibut fillets. Skin-on fillets work best, so you can serve the deliciously crisp roasted skin. Use a heavy-duty pan to help keep the fillets from sticking to the pan.

- 4 bass fillets, each about 7 ounces (195 g) and ¾-inch thick
- ¼ cup (65 g) refrigerated or jarred red pesto
- 2 ounces (55 g) pancetta or bacon, chopped
- 1 tablespoon (8.6 g) drained capers
- 1 lemon, cut into wedges

Preheat the broiler.

Pat dry the fish with paper towels and arrange skin-side down in a large ovenproof pan or baking sheet (preferably nonstick). Spread the pesto over the top of the fillets and scatter on the bacon and capers.

Broil about 4 inches (10 cm) from the heat until the fish is just a bit filmy and moist in the thickest part when checked with a fork, 4 to 5 minutes.

Serve with the lemon wedges for squeezing.

Prep = 5 minutes   **Cook** = 5 minutes
Yield = 4 servings

Scrod with Spicy Tomato Prosciutto Sauce

Young cod is known as scrod and weighs about 2 pounds (1 kg) or less. If you can't find it, use haddock. Here, the fish is baked in a piquant sauce inspired by the famous "Biscayne" tomato sauce from the Basque region of Spain.

- 3 tablespoons (42 g) butter
- 2 cups (260 g) prechopped onion
- ½ cup (120 g) jarred roasted red peppers, drained and chopped
- 2 tablespoons (18 g) chopped prosciutto
- 1 teaspoon preminced oil-packed garlic
- 1 tablespoon (9 g) ancho chili powder
- ¼ teaspoon sugar
- 1 cup (250 g) refrigerated or jarred tomato sauce with garlic and onion
- 1½ pounds (680 g) scrod (young cod) fillets
  Salt and ground black pepper

Melt the butter in a medium saucepan over medium heat. Add the onions and cook until golden, 5 to 7 minutes. Add the roasted peppers, prosciutto, garlic, ancho powder, and sugar. Cook for 2 minutes. Stir in the tomato sauce and cook until the flavors blend, about 5 minutes. Puree with a hand blender or in a food processor or blender.

Preheat the oven to 425ºF (220ºC, or gas mark 7).

Spread a few tablespoons of the sauce over the bottom of a 2½-quart (2.5-L) baking dish. Lightly season the fish with salt and black pepper. Arrange the fillets in the dish and spoon the remaining sauce over the top. Cover with foil and bake until the fish is just a bit filmy and moist in the center, 8 to 10 minutes. Serve the fish with the pan juices.

Prep = 5 minutes   **Cook** = 25 minutes
Yield = 4 servings

Spinach-Stuffed Flounder with Cheddar Dill Sauce

Doctored-up prepared cheese sauce makes this diner favorite a snap to whip up at home. Serve with herbed rice.

- 1 cup (230 g) refrigerated or jarred cheddar cheese sauce
- 1¼ cups (145 g) preshreaded sharp cheddar cheese
- ½ teaspoon dried dill
- 1 tablespoon (14 g) butter
- ¼ cup (33 g) prechopped onion, finely chopped
- 1 cup (130 g) prechopped red bell peppers, finely chopped
- 2 teaspoons preminced oil-packed garlic
- 6 ounces (about 4 cups, or 170 g) washed baby spinach leaves
- ¼ cup (30 g) seasoned dried bread crumbs
- 1 pound (455 g) flounder fillets, at least ½-inch thick at the wide end
- Salt and ground black pepper

Preheat the oven to 425°F (220°C, or gas mark 7).

Combine the cheese sauce, cheese, and dill into a small saucepan. Heat over medium heat until the cheese melts. Spread a few tablespoons of the mixture over the bottom of a 2-quart (2-L) baking dish. Set aside.

Heat the 1 tablespoon butter (14 g) in a large skillet over medium-high heat. Add the onions and bell peppers and cook until softened, about 4 minutes. Add the garlic and cook for 1 minute. Stir in the spinach and cook until wilted and most of the liquid evaporates, 2 to 3 minutes. Stir in 2 tablespoons (28 g) of the cheese sauce and the bread crumbs. Remove from the heat.

Cut the fillets in half lengthwise and lightly season with salt and ground black pepper. Spoon 2 tablespoons of the spinach mixture near the thick end of each piece of fish. Roll toward the thin end and secure with toothpicks if necessary. Put the rolls seam-side down in the prepared dish. Pour the remaining cheese sauce over top.

Prep = 5 minutes   **Cook** = 25 minutes
Yield = 4 servings

Braised Grouper Puttanesca

Puttanesca generally refers to tomato sauce with plenty of add-ins like olives, capers, and sun-dried tomatoes.

1½ to 2	pounds (680 g to 1 kg) skinless grouper fillets
	Salt and ground black pepper
¼	cup (30 g) all-purpose flour
3	tablespoons (43 ml) olive oil
1	cup (130 g) prechopped onion
1	tablespoon (10 g) preminced oil-packed garlic
¼	teaspoon crushed red pepper flakes
½	cup (120 ml) dry white wine
1	teaspoon anchovy paste or 1 large anchovy fillet, finely chopped
⅓	cup (30 g) pitted kalamata olives
¼	cup (13 g) oil-packed sun-dried tomato strips or bits
1	jar (26 ounces, or 737 g) tomato sauce with garlic and onion

Lightly season the fish with salt and black pepper. Roll in the flour to coat, patting off the excess. Heat the oil in a large skillet over medium-high heat. Add the fish and cook until browned all over, 2 to 3 minutes per side. Carefully remove to a plate with a spatula.

Add the onions to the pan and cook until golden, about 4 minutes. Add the garlic and red pepper flakes and cook 1 minute. Add the wine and cook, scraping the pan bottom, until the liquid reduces in volume by about half, 3 to 4 minutes. Stir in the anchovy paste, olives, and sun-dried tomatoes. Reduce the heat to medium-low and stir in the tomato sauce. Bring to a simmer then return the fish to the pan, spooning some sauce over the top. Cover and simmer gently until the fish is just a bit filmy and moist in the center when checked with a fork, 10 to 15 minutes.

Prep = 3 minutes **Cook** = 25 minutes **Yield** = 4 servings

Scallop and Mushroom Gratin

3	slices sandwich bread
¼	cup (15 g) packed parsley leaves
5	tablespoons (70 g) butter, melted
½	cup (50 g) grated Parmesan cheese
	Salt and ground black pepper
½	cup (65 g) prechopped onion
1	tablespoon (10 g) preminced oil-packed garlic
10	ounces (280 g) presliced cremini or white mushrooms
¾	cup (175 ml) dry white wine or vermouth
1½	cups (375 g) refrigerated or jarred Alfredo sauce
1½	pounds (680 g) sea scallops, quartered

Pulse the bread and parsley in a food processor until the mixture is reduced to coarse crumbs. With the motor running, add 3 tablespoons (42 g) of the butter through the feed tube and process just until mixed. Lightly season with salt and black pepper. Set aside.

Melt the remaining 2 tablespoons (28 g) butter in a large skillet over medium heat. Add the onions and cook until soft, 2 to 3 minutes. Add the garlic and mushrooms and cook until the mushrooms give off most of their liquid, about 5 minutes. Add the wine and boil over high heat until the liquid is reduced in volume by about half, 5 minutes. Reduce the heat to medium and stir in the Alfredo sauce.

Preheat the broiler. Stir the scallops into the pan, spooning some sauce over them. Simmer gently until the scallops are barely translucent in the center, about 2 minutes. Remove from the heat and spoon the mixture into six 3-ounce (85-g) ramekins, a 1½-quart (1.5-L) gratin dish, or a 9-inch (22.5-cm) deep-dish pie plate. Put dish(es) on a baking sheet and scatter the bread crumb mixture over the top. Broil 4 inches (10 cm) from the heat until golden brown, 1 to 2 minutes.

Prep = 5 minutes **Cook** = 18 minutes   **Yield** = 4 to 6 servings

Baked Salmon on Pesto Potato Pancakes

Moist seafood atop crispy pancakes—the combination is irresistible. The pancakes are also delicious on their own as a side dish with roast chicken or pork.

- 3 cups (9 ounces, or 255 g) frozen mashed potatoes, thawed
- ½ cup (65 g) prechopped onion, minced
- 5 tablespoons (80 g) refrigerated or jarred basil pesto sauce, divided
- 1 egg, beaten
- ½ teaspoon ground black pepper
- 2 tablespoons (28 ml) olive oil
- 2 pounds (1 kg) boneless, skinless salmon fillets, cut into 6 equal portions

Preheat the oven to 375°F (190°C, or gas mark 5). Coat a large baking sheet with vegetable oil spray. Set aside.

In a bowl, combine the potatoes, onion, 4 tablespoons (64 g) pesto, egg, and pepper. Shape into 6 oval patties about ¼-inch thick. Place on the prepared sheet and bake until the edges start to brown, about 15 minutes.

Meanwhile, in a small bowl, whisk the oil with the remaining 1 tablespoon (16 g) pesto. Remove the pan from the oven. Place a salmon fillet atop each patty. Drizzle with the pesto oil. Bake until the salmon is opaque, about 12 minutes.

Prep = 5 minutes   **Cook** = 17 minutes
Yield = 6 servings

Poached Salmon with Rosemary Sun-Dried Tomato Sauce

Most home cooks don't make fish stock. Here's a quick version using bottled clam juice, chicken broth, and wine. This blend makes a fair substitute, especially when mixed with other ingredients to create a simple poaching liquid for salmon.

- 2 tablespoons (28 ml) olive oil
- ½ cup (65 g) prechopped onion
- 2 teaspoons preminced oil-packed garlic
- ½ cup (120 ml) dry white wine or vermouth
- 1 cup (235 ml) bottled clam juice
- ½ cup (120 ml) low-sodium chicken broth
- 1 cup (250 g) refrigerated or jarred marinara tomato sauce
- ¼ teaspoon crushed red pepper flakes
- 1½ pounds (680 g) salmon fillets, cut into 4 portions
- ¼ cup (25 g) pitted kalamata olives
- 2 tablespoons (6 g) oil-packed sun-dried tomato bits
- 1 tablespoon (8.6 g) drained capers
- 2 teaspoons chopped fresh rosemary

Prep = 2 minutess   **Cook** = 35 minutes
Yield = 4 servings

Heat the oil in a large, deep skillet over medium-high heat. Add the onions and cook until golden, 2 to 3 minutes. Add the garlic and cook 1 minute. Add the wine or vermouth and simmer 2 minutes. Add the clam juice and broth. Reduce the heat to medium and simmer until the liquid is reduced in volume by about one-third.

Stir in the tomato sauce and red pepper flakes, and simmer over medium heat until the flavors are blended, 5 to 8 minutes. Puree in an upright blender or food processor. Return to a simmer over medium heat. Add the salmon skin-side up, cover, and simmer gently for 5 minutes. Carefully invert the salmon with a spatula, cover, and simmer until the salmon is just a bit filmy and moist in the center when checked with a fork, an additional 5 to 7 minutes. Remove the fish to soup plates and cover with foil to keep warm.

Add the olives, sun-dried tomato bits, capers, and rosemary to the liquid in the pan. Bring to a boil over high heat, then reduce the heat to medium and simmer for 5 minutes. Serve over the salmon.

Shrimp Rémoulade Salad

Precooked potatoes, which are available in the produce section of some supermarkets, make this dish super-quick to prepare. If unavailable, simply microwave small new potatoes in a single layer on a microwaveable plate until fork tender, about five minutes on high power.

¾ cup (188 g) refrigerated or jarred Alfredo sauce
1½ tablespoons (23 g) Creole or Dijon mustard
1½ tablespoons (13 g) drained and rinsed capers
½ teaspoon ground black pepper
1½ pounds (680 g) peeled cooked medium shrimp
¾ pound (340 g) precooked new potatoes, diced
¾ cup (120 g) prechopped celery
6 cups (6 ounces, or 170 g) prewashed spring salad mix
1 bunch scallions, white and light green parts, sliced (⅓ cup, or 33 g)

In a mixing bowl, combine the sauce, mustard, capers, and pepper. Add the shrimp, potatoes, and celery. Toss to coat. Arrange the greens on plates. Spoon the shrimp mixture over the greens and garnish with the scallions.

Prep = 6 minutes   **Yield** = 4 to 6 servings

Wasabi-Crusted Tuna with Creamy Red Pepper Sauce

Seared tuna is simple to make at home. Look for the best-quality 1-inch (2.5-cm)-thick tuna steaks you can find. Wasabi powder is available near the soy sauce in the Asian section of most grocery stores.

- ½ cup (75 g) wasabi powder
- ½ cup (120 ml) water
- 1 teaspoon salt
- 2 tablespoons (28 ml) olive oil
- 1 cup (120 g) drained jarred roasted red peppers
- ¾ cup (188 g) refrigerated or jarred sundried tomato Alfredo sauce
- 4 tuna steaks, each about 7 ounces (195 g) and 1-inch (2.5-cm) thick

Combine the wasabi powder, water, and salt in a small bowl. Let stand for 10 minutes to develop flavors. Add water, 1 tablespoon at a time to create a runny sauce. Pat dry the tuna with paper towels and coat both sides with the wasabi mixture.

Heat 1 tablespoon (14 ml) of the oil in a small saucepan over medium heat. Add the roasted red peppers and cook for 2 minutes. Stir in the Alfredo sauce and water and cook 2 minutes. Puree with a hand blender or in an upright blender. Reduce the heat to low and keep warm.

Heat the remaining 1 tablespoon (14 ml) oil in a large, heavy skillet over high heat. Add the tuna and sear until well browned on both sides and red at the core (medium-rare), about 3 minutes per side.

Spoon the sauce onto the plates and top with the tuna.

Prep = 3 minutes **Cook** = 12 minutes
Yield = 4 servings

Fried Tuna Cakes

Similar to crab cakes, these tuna cakes pair well with tartar sauce. Or, make a flavored mayonnaise by mixing ½ cup (112 g) jarred mayonnaise with 2 tablespoons (17 g) drained and chopped capers, 1 tablespoon (14 ml) olive oil, and the juice of half a lemon.

- 4 cans (6 ounces, or 170 g, each) water- or oil-packed tuna, drained
- ¾ cup (188 g) refrigerated or jarred sun-dried tomato Alfredo sauce
- 1 egg
- 1 scallion, minced
- 3 tablespoons (12 g) chopped fresh parsley
- 1½ teaspoons prepared mustard
- ½ teaspoon hot pepper sauce
- 2 cups (230 g) seasoned dry bread crumbs
- 1 lemon
- ½ cup (120 ml) vegetable oil

Crumble the fish into a bowl and stir in the Alfredo sauce, egg, scallion, parsley, mustard, hot pepper sauce and ¾ cup (87 g) of the bread crumbs. Cut the lemon in half and squeeze the juice from one half into the bowl. Mix well. Cut the remaining lemon into wedges.

Put the remaining 1¼ cups (143 g) bread crumbs in a shallow bowl. Shape the tuna mixture into 3-inch (7.5-cm) patties (about 14). Roll the patties in the bread crumbs to coat.

Heat half of the oil in a large skillet over medium heat. When hot, add half of the patties and cook until browned on both sides, 3 to 4 minutes per side. Repeat with the remaining oil and patties.

Serve with the lemon wedges.

Prep = 15 minutes   **Cook** = 8 minutes
Yield = 6 servings

Clams Filipino

Kitchen magic happens when a handful of prepared ingredients are simmered together to create this exotic sauce for tiny sweet clams. The sauce can be prepared well in advance— even refrigerated—and the clams cooked in it just before serving.

½ cup (65 g) prechopped onion
2 tablespoons (28 ml) vegetable oil
2 teaspoons preminced oil-packed garlic
1 teaspoon ground turmeric
1 teaspoon refrigerated pregrated fresh ginger
1 cup (250 g) refrigerated or jarred tomato marinara sauce with mushrooms
1½ cups (355 ml) water
¼ cup (60 ml) soy sauce, preferably low-sodium
100 littleneck clams (about 7 pounds, or 195 g)

In a large pot over medium-low heat, combine the onion, oil, garlic, turmeric, and ginger. Cook, stirring, until the onion is soft, about 5 minutes. Add the tomato sauce, water, and soy sauce. Increase the heat to high. Bring the mixture to a boil. Add the clams. Stir. Cover and cook, stirring occasionally, until the clams open, about 6 minutes. Serve in large bowls with the sauce.

Prep = 5 minutes   **Cook** = 12 minutes   **Yield** = 4 to 6 servings

Mussels in Orange Saffron Sauce

Make this dish and the intoxicating floral aromas of saffron and sweet citrus will perfume your kitchen. Serve with lemon wedges for squeezing and crusty bread to soak up the irresistible sauce.

- 1 tablespoon (14 ml) olive oil
- ½ cup (65 g) prechopped onion
- 2 teaspoons preminced oil-packed garlic
- 2 oranges
- ¼ cup (42 g) dry sherry
- ½ cup (120 ml) orange juice
- ¾ cup (188 g) refrigerated or jarred tomato basil sauce
- ¼ teaspoon crushed saffron threads
- ¼ cup (15 g) chopped fresh parsley
- 4 pounds (2 kg, or about 4 dozen) mussels, scrubbed and debearded

Heat the oil in a large pot or large, deep skillet over medium heat. When hot, add the onions and cook until soft, 2 to 3 minutes. Add the garlic and cook 1 minute. Grate the zest from 1 of the oranges into the pan. Cut both oranges in half and squeeze the juice into the pan. Stir in the sherry, orange juice, tomato sauce, saffron, and parsley. Bring to a boil over high heat. Add the mussels, spooning some sauce over the top. Cover and boil, shaking the pan now and then, until the mussels open, 5 to 7 minutes. Discard any unopened mussels. Using a slotted spoon, remove the mussels to a serving bowl.

Using a fine mesh strainer, strain the cooking liquid over the mussels.

Prep = 3 minutes   **Cook** = 12 minutes   **Yield** = Makes 4 servings

5 INGREDIENTS OR LESS

15 MINUTES OR LESS

Cajun Oysters

When shucking fresh oysters, work over
a bowl to save the oyster liquid (liquor) that
dribbles out of the shells. Strain the oyster
liquor to remove any bits of broken shell.
This mini-meal can be made more substantial
simply by doubling the recipe.

16   large fresh oysters, shucked (oyster liquor reserved)
1   cup (250 g) refrigerated or jarred Alfredo sauce
2 to 3   teaspoons hot pepper sauce
2   large croissants, halved and hollowed out in the center
4   teaspoons caviar (optional)

Pour ¼ cup (60 ml) of the reserved oyster liquor in a large
skillet. Add the oysters and simmer until plump, about 30
seconds. Using a slotted spoon, remove the oysters to a plate
and cover to keep warm. Cook the liquid in the pan over
medium-high heat until reduced to about ¼ cup (60 ml), 2 to
3 minutes. Reduce the heat to medium-low and stir in the
Alfredo sauce and hot pepper sauce. Cook 1 minute, then
return the oysters to the pan and heat through.

    Spoon the mixture evenly into the croissants. Top each
serving with 1 teaspoon caviar, if using.

Prep = 10 minutes   **Cook** = 5 minutes   **Yield** = 4 modest servings

Sicilian
Halibut Steaks

Sicilians generally prefer assertive flavors
such as the acidity of balsamic vinegar
contrasted with the sweetness of oranges
and honey.

1	small fennel bulb (about 8 ounces, or 225 g)
2	tablespoons (28 ml) olive oil
1½	cups (195 g) prechopped onion
1	tablespoon (10 g) preminced oil-packed garlic
1	small orange
1	tablespoon (14 ml) balsamic vinegar
1	tablespoon (20 g) honey
3	tablespoons (30 g) raisins
1½	teaspoons chopped fresh mint or ½ teaspoon dried
2	cups (250 g) refrigerated or jarred marinara tomato sauce
4	halibut steaks (about 1½ pounds, or 680 g, total)
	Salt and ground black pepper

Remove and discard the fibrous light green stems from the
fennel bulb. Reserve 2 tablespoons (8 g) dark green feathery
leaves. Quarter the white bulb and slice thinly.

Heat the oil in a large skillet over medium-high heat. Add
the onions and fennel and cook until the onions are golden,
4 to 6 minutes. Add the garlic and cook for 1 minute. Grate
the zest from half the orange into the pan. Cut the orange in
half and squeeze all of the juice into the pan. Stir in the balsamic vinegar and simmer until the liquid reduces slightly,
about 2 minutes. Stir in the honey, raisins, mint, and tomato
sauce. Reduce the heat to medium-low and cook until the flavors have blended, 5 to 8 minutes.

Preheat the oven to 425ºF (220°C, or gas mark 7).

Spread a few tablespoons of the sauce over the bottom of
a 2½-quart (2.5-L) baking dish. Lightly season the fish with
salt and black pepper. Arrange the fish in the dish and spoon
the remaining sauce over the top. Bake uncovered until the
fish is just a bit filmy and moist in the center when checked
with a fork, about 15 minutes.

Prep = 10 minutes   **Cook** = 30 minutes   **Yield** = 4 servings

Pasta Dishes

Creamy Rotini Salad with Broccoli and Tomatoes

Better than mayonnaise? Alfredo sauce tastes even more decadent than mayonnaise in this dressing, but surprisingly contains less than one-third of the calories and only one-quarter of the fat.

4   cups (12 ounces, or 340 g) dried rotini pasta
1   bag (8 ounces, or 225 g) broccoli florets, chopped
¾   cup (188 g) refrigerated or jarred Alfredo sauce
1   tablespoon (14 ml) red or white wine vinegar
½   teaspoon ground black pepper
1   pint (2 cups, or 600 g) grape tomatoes, halved
¾   cup (30 g) shredded fresh basil
¼   cup (33 g) finely chopped red onion
⅓   cup (45 g) pine nuts, toasted

Cook the pasta according to the package directions and add the broccoli 1 minute before draining. Drain the pasta and broccoli and rinse well with cold running water. Set aside.

In a large bowl, combine the sauce, vinegar, and pepper. Whisk to combine. Add the tomatoes, basil, onion, and reserved rotini and broccoli. Toss. Scatter on the nuts.

Prep = 5 minutes   **Cook** = 6 minutes   **Yield** = 4 to 6 servings

Angel Hair with Scallops, Spinach, and Vodka Sauce

The fastest way to boil pasta is to start with hot tap water and keep the pot covered so that the water quickly returns to a boil. For a simple garnish here, toast about 3 tablespoons (24 g) pine nuts in the skillet before adding any oil. Scatter the toasted nuts over the top with some grated Asiago or Grana Padano cheese.

12	ounces (340 g) angel hair pasta
¼	cup (60 ml) olive oil
1	pound (455 g) small sea scallops
	Salt and ground black pepper
½	cup (65 g) prechopped onion
1	tablespoon (10 g) preminced oil-packed garlic
½	cup (120 ml) dry white wine or vermouth
1½	cups (375 g) refrigerated or jarred vodka tomato sauce with cream
6	ounces (170 g) washed baby spinach leaves

Prep = 2 minutes   **Cook** = 13 minutes   **Yield** = 4 servings

Cook the pasta according to the package directions.

Heat 2 tablespoons (28 ml) of the oil in a large skillet over medium-high heat. Lightly season the scallops with salt and pepper, then add to the hot pan. Cook until browned on both sides, 1 to 2 minutes per side. Remove to a plate.

Heat another tablespoon (14 ml) of the oil in the pan and add the onions. Cook until golden, 2 to 3 minutes. Add the garlic and cook 1 minute. Add the wine or vermouth and cook until the liquid reduces slightly, about 2 minutes. Stir in the vodka sauce and reduce the heat to medium-low. Return the scallops to the pan along with the spinach. Cook until the scallops are barely translucent in the center and the spinach is wilted, about 1 minute.

Drain the pasta and toss with the remaining 1 tablespoon (14 ml) oil. Arrange on plates and top with the tomato mixture and scallops.

Pesto Spaghetti with Asparagus and Shrimp

This fresh and light dish makes a perfect springtime supper. Pass a few lemon wedges for squeezing at the table.

12 ounces (340 g) thin spaghetti or other thin-strand pasta
8 ounces (225 g) asparagus, trimmed and cut into 1 ½-inch (3.75cm) lengths
1 pound (455 g) peeled, deveined medium shrimp, thawed if frozen
Salt and ground black pepper
1 lemon
½ cup (130 g) refrigerated or jarred basil pesto
¼ cup (60 ml) olive oil
1 tablespoon (10 g) preminced oil-packed garlic

Cook the pasta according to the package directions.

Meanwhile, lightly season the asparagus and shrimp with salt and pepper. Grate the zest from the lemon over the asparagus and shrimp. Cut the lemon in half and squeeze the juice into a bowl. Stir in the pesto and 3 tablespoons (42 ml) of the olive oil.

Heat the remaining 1 tablespoon (14 ml) oil in a large skillet over medium-high heat. Add the asparagus and cook for 2 minutes. Add the shrimp and garlic and cook until the shrimp are bright pink and the asparagus is crisp-tender, 2 minutes more.

Drain the pasta and toss with the pesto mixture in the pasta pot. Divide among pasta plates and spoon the asparagus and shrimp over the top.

Prep = 3 minutes   **Cook** = 12 minutes   **Yield** = 4 servings

Linguine with Walnuts and Blue Cheese

Alfredo sauce, walnuts, and Gorgonzola cheese create a lusciously rich sauce for linguine or fettuccine. Serve with a green salad.

- 12 ounces (340 g) linguine or fettuccine
- 2 tablespoons (28 ml) extra-virgin olive oil
- ¾ cup (90 g) chopped walnuts
- 1 tablespoon (10 g) preminced oil-packed garlic
- 1¼ cups (300 g) refrigerated or jarred Alfredo sauce
- ½ cup (120 ml) milk
- ¼ cup (15 g) chopped fresh parsley
- ¼ cup (30 g) crumbled Gorgonzola or other creamy cheese

Cook the pasta according to the package directions.

Meanwhile, heat the oil in a large skillet over medium heat. Add the walnuts and garlic and cook until fragrant but not browned, 4 to 6 minutes. Reduce the heat to medium-low and stir in the Alfredo sauce, ½ cup of the milk, and 3 tablespoons (12 g) of the parsley. Cook until heated through, 2 minutes. Add more milk if necessary to thin the sauce. Drain the pasta and add to the sauce, stirring to coat completely. Divide among pasta plates and scatter the Gorgonzola over top. Garnish with the remaining 1 tablespoon (4 g) parsley.

Prep = 5 minutes   **Cook** = 8 minutes   **Yield** = 4 servings

Shrimp Pad Thai

With bottled marinara sauce as the
flavor base, this exotic noodle stir-fry
comes together fast. Thin strips
of chicken or pork can
take the place of the shrimp.

12	ounces (340 g) Thai-style flat rice noodles
1	cup (250 g) refrigerated or jarred tomato marinara sauce
¼	cup (60 ml) Asian fish sauce or soy sauce
2	tablespoons (28 g) brown sugar
3	tablespoons (42 ml) vegetable oil
1	pound (455 g) peeled, deveined medium shrimp, thawed if frozen
3	teaspoons preminced oil-packed garlic
2	eggs, beaten
1	cup (60 g) fresh cilantro leaves
¼	cup (30 g) finely chopped dry-roasted peanuts
1	lime, cut into wedges
	Asian hot chili sauce

Soak the noodles according to the package directions.
In a bowl, whisk the marinara, fish or soy sauce, and sugar.
Set aside.

In a wok or large skillet, heat 1 tablespoon (14 ml) oil over
high heat. Add the shrimp and 1 teaspoon garlic. Cook, tossing, until opaque, about 2 minutes. Remove to a plate.

Add the remaining 2 tablespoons (28 ml) oil to the wok or
skillet set over high heat. Drain the noodles and add to the
pan with the remaining 2 teaspoons garlic. Toss to coat with
oil, about 1 minute. Add the reserved sauce mixture. Toss
for 1 minute to heat. Add the eggs. Toss for 2 minutes or until
the sauce mixture thickens. Add the shrimp and toss
to reheat.

Garnish with the cilantro and peanuts. Pass the lime and
chili sauce at the table.

Prep = 12 minutes **Cook** = 8 minutes
Yield = 4 to 6 servings

5 INGREDIENTS OR LESS

15 MINUTES OR LESS

Linguine with Sausage and Arugula

Some nights call for super-quick pasta. Doctoring up vodka sauce with fresh arugula and Italian sausage makes ordinary linguine something special.

- 8 ounces (225 g) loose-pack Italian sausage
- 12 ounces (340 g) linguine or spaghetti
- 6 cups (6 ounces, or 170 g) baby arugula
- 1 cup (250 g) refrigerated or jarred vodka tomato sauce with cream
- 3 tablespoons (7.5 g) chopped fresh basil, optional

Scatter chunks of the sausage in a large cold skillet set over medium heat. Add about 2 tablespoons (28 ml) water to the pan. Cook, flipping occasionally with a spatula, until browned, about 7 minutes.

Meanwhile, cook the pasta according to the package directions.

Add the arugula to the sausage in the pan. Cook, stirring, until wilted, about 2 minutes. Add the sauce and keep warm at a low simmer.

Drain the linguine. Add to the skillet and toss to coat with sauce. Garnish with the basil, if using.

Prep = 3 minutes   **Cook** = 12 minutes
Yield = 4 to 6 servings

Shells with Lentils and Broccoli Rabe

When trimming broccoli rabe, cut off the tough, woody ends and remove any wilted or yellowed leaves.

- ¾ cup (170 g) brown lentils, picked over and rinsed
- 1½ cups 355 ml) low-sodium chicken broth
- 12 ounces (340 g) medium shell pasta
- 2 tablespoons (28 ml) olive oil
- 2 cups (260 g) prechopped onion
- 8 ounces (225 g) presliced cremini or white mushrooms
- 1 tablespoon (10 g) preminced oil-packed garlic
- 1 teaspoon crushed dried rosemary
- ⅛ to ¼ teaspoon crushed red pepper flakes
- ¼ cup (60 ml) dry red wine or chicken broth
- 12 ounces (340 g) broccoli rabe, trimmed and cut into 2-inch (5-cm) lengths
- 2 cups (500 g) refrigerated or jarred tomato marinara sauce with red wine
- ¼ cup (25 g) grated Parmesan cheese

Put the lentils and broth in a medium saucepan. Cover and bring to a boil over high heat. Reduce the heat to medium-low and simmer until the lentils are tender, about 15 minutes.

Meanwhile, cook the pasta according to the package.

Heat the oil in a large skillet over medium-high heat. Add the onions and cook until golden, about 4 minutes. Add the mushrooms, garlic, rosemary, and red pepper flakes. Cook until the mushrooms begin to release their liquid, about 5 minutes. Add the wine or chicken broth and broccoli rabe. Simmer, scraping the pan bottom, until the liquid nearly evaporates, 2 to 3 minutes. Add the marinara sauce and reduce the heat to medium-low. Cook until the flavors have blended and the broccoli rabe is crisp-tender, about 5 minutes. Stir in the lentils along with their cooking liquid.

Drain the pasta and add to the sauce, mixing thouroughly. Divide among pasta plates and garnish with the Parmesan.

Prep = 8 minutes   **Cook** = 20 minutes
Yield = 4 to 6 servings

Thai Fettuccine Primavera

Look for Thai red curry base in large packets in the international aisle or Asian section of your grocery store.

1 pound (455 g) fettuccine
2 tablespoons (28 ml) olive oil
2 cups (140 g) broccoli florets
1 cup (110 g) presliced onion
1½ cups (180 g) presliced bell peppers (red and yellow)
1 tablespoon (8 g) jarred pregrated fresh ginger
1 tablespoon (10 g) preminced oil-packed garlic
1 can (14 ounces, or 425 ml) coconut milk
1 cup (250 g) refrigerated or jarred Alfredo sauce
2 tablespoons (30 g) Thai red curry base
1 tablespoon (14 g) brown sugar
¼ cup (30 g) chopped peanuts
¼ cup (15 g) chopped fresh cilantro or basil
1 lime, cut into small wedges

Cook the pasta according to the package directions.

Meanwhile, heat the oil in a large, deep skillet over medium-high heat. Add the broccoli and cook for 1 to 2 minutes. Add the onions and cook an additional 1 minute. Add the bell peppers, ginger, and garlic, and cook until the vegetables are crisp-tender, 1 to 2 minutes more. Remove to a plate and cover to keep warm.

Add the coconut milk, Alfredo sauce, red curry base, and brown sugar to the pan. Bring to a boil, whisking or stirring until thoroughly mixed, then reduce the heat to medium and simmer for 3 to 5 minutes.

Drain the pasta and mix with about ¾ cup of the curry sauce. Stir the vegetables back into the remaining sauce.

Divide the pasta among plates and top with the vegetables and sauce. Sprinkle with the peanuts and cilantro or basil. Serve with the lime wedges for squeezing.

Prep = 3 minutes   **Cook** = 12 minutes
Yield = 4 servings

Orecchiette with Pancetta and Peas

Orecchiette or "little ears" have little cavities that perfectly cradle the peas and bacon bits in this dish. If orecchiette are unavailable, use small shell pasta or a long-strand pasta such as spaghetti or linguine. Garnish the dish with chopped fresh parsley if you like.

12 ounces (340 g) orecchiette or small shells
4   ounces (115 g) pancetta or thick bacon
    (3 to 4 slices), finely chopped
⅛   teaspoon crushed saffron threads, optional
1¼ cups (300 g) refrigerated or jarred Alfredo sauce
½   cup (65 g) frozen peas, thawed

Cook the pasta according to the package directions. Meanwhile, put the pancetta or bacon and saffron (if using) in a medium skillet over medium heat. Cook until the bacon is crisp, about 5 minutes.

Reduce the heat to medium-low and add the Alfredo sauce and peas. Cook until heated through, 3 to 4 minutes. Drain the pasta and toss with ½ cup of the sauce. Divide among pasta plates and spoon the remaining sauce over top.

Prep = 3 minutes **Cook** = 12 minutes **Yield** = 4 to 6 servings

Penne with Ricotta and Broccolini

Broccolini (baby broccoli) is a skinny broccoli hybrid that's increasingly available in grocery store produce sections. If you can't find it, use broccoli florets or asparagus. Chopped fresh basil makes the perfect garnish.

1	pound (455 g) penne or other short-shape pasta
2	tablespoons (28 ml) olive oil
1½	pounds (680 g) broccolini, trimmed and cut into 1½ -inch (3.75-cm) lengths
2	teaspoons anchovy paste or 4 anchovy fillets, mashed
2	teaspoons preminced oil-packed garlic
½	teaspoon crushed red pepper flakes
1	cup (8 ounces, or 225 g) ricotta cheese
1	cup (250 g) refrigerated or jarred Alfredo sauce
¾	cup (175 ml) milk

Cook the pasta according to the package directions.
  Meanwhile, heat the oil in a large skillet and cook over medium-high heat. Add the broccolini, cover, and cook for 3 minutes, shaking the pan once or twice. Uncover and add the anchovy paste, garlic, and red pepper flakes. Cook 1 minute. Reduce the heat to medium and stir in the ricotta, Alfredo sauce, and milk. Mix well and cook until heated through and the broccolini is crisp-tender, 3 to 4 minutes.
  Drain the pasta and toss with the sauce.

Prep = 2 minutes   **Cook** = 12 minutes   **Yield** = 6 servings

Spicy Penne with Shrimp

If you hate to chop, here's your dish. It uses precut produce and precooked bacon to keep prep and cooking times to a minimum. Garnish with pregrated Parmesan.

12	ounces (340 g) penne or other short-shape pasta
1	tablespoon (14 ml) olive oil
6	strips (1½ ounces, or 43 g) precooked bacon
1	cup (130 g) prechopped onion
1	tablespoon (10 g) preminced oil-packed garlic
¼	teaspoon crushed red pepper flakes
½	cup (120 ml) dry white wine
1	pound (455 g) medium peeled and deveined shrimp, thawed if frozen
1½	cups (375 g) refrigerated or jarred tomato sauce with onion and garlic

Cook the pasta according to the package directions.

Meanwhile, heat the oil in a large skillet over medium heat. Add the bacon and cook until sizzling, about 2 minutes. Remove to a paper-towel-lined plate.

Increase the heat to medium-high and add the onions to the pan. Cook until golden, about 4 minutes. Add the garlic and pepper flakes, and cook 1 minute. Add the wine and shrimp and simmer until the shrimp begin to turn pink, 1 to 2 minutes. Add the tomato sauce and cook until heated through and the shrimp are bright pink, 2 to 3 minutes.

Drain the pasta and toss with ¾ cup of the sauce. Divide the pasta among pasta plates and serve the shrimp and remaining sauce over top. Crumble the bacon over each serving.

Prep = 2 minutes **Cook** = 13 minutes **Yield** = 4 servings

Bow Ties
with Chicken and
Mushrooms

Chicken, mushrooms, and Alfredo sauce make a supremely comforting combination. A bit of thyme and white wine heighten the flavors.

- 12 ounces (340 g) bow-tie pasta
- 1 pound (455 g) chicken tenders, white tendons removed, cut into 2-inch (5-cm)-long strips
- Salt and pepper
- 2 tablespoons (28 ml) olive oil
- 1 pound (455 g) presliced cremini or white mushrooms
- 1 tablespoon (10 g) preminced oil-packed garlic
- 1 teaspoon dried thyme
- ½ cup (120 ml) dry white wine or sherry
- 1½ cups (375 g) refrigerated or jarred Alfredo sauce
- ¼ cup (15 g) chopped fresh parsley

Cook the pasta according to the package directions.

Meanwhile, lightly season the chicken with salt and pepper. Heat the oil in a large skillet over medium-high heat. Add the chicken and cook until no longer pink, about 5 minutes, turning once or twice. Remove to a plate and cover to keep warm.

Add the mushrooms, garlic, and thyme to the pan. Cook until the mushrooms begin to release their liquid, about 5 minutes. Add the wine and simmer, scraping the pan bottom, until the liquid is almost gone, 3 to 4 minutes.

Reduce the heat to low and add the Alfredo sauce and 2 tablespoons (8 g) of the parsley. Return the chicken to the pan and heat through, 2 to 3 minutes.

Drain the pasta and mix with ½ cup of the sauce to moisten. Divide among pasta plates and spoon the sauce over top. Scatter on the remaining parsley.

Prep = 10 minutes   **Cook** = 15 minutes   **Yield** = 4 servings

Ziti with Green Beans and Bacon

Crumbled bacon and provolone cheese add deep flavors to this simple pasta toss. Penne or rotini can stand in for the ziti if you like.

4   cups (12 ounces, or 340 g) dried ziti pasta
1   bag (8 ounces, or 225 g) pretrimmed green beans, broken into ½-inch pieces
1   tablespoon (14 ml) olive oil
6   strips (1½ ounces, or 43 g) precooked bacon
¾   cup (3 ounces, or 85 g) prechopped onion
2   teaspoons preminced oil-packed garlic
1   cup (250 g) refrigerated or jarred tomato sauce with four cheeses
¾   cup (3 ounces, or 85 g) preshredded provolone cheese

Cook the pasta according to the package directions, adding the green beans to the pot at the same time.

Meanwhile, heat the oil in a large skillet over medium heat. Add the bacon and cook until sizzling, about 2 minutes. Remove the bacon to a paper-towel-lined plate. Add the onion and garlic to the pan. Cook, stirring, until golden, about 5 minutes. Add the sauce. Keep warm at a low simmer.

Before draining the ziti, reserve ½ cup (120 ml) of the cooking water. Drain the ziti and beans. Return to the pot. Add the sauce. Toss to coat. Add some of the reserved water if the sauce is too thick. Add the cheese and toss to melt. Crumble the bacon and sprinkle over the pasta.

Prep = 3 minutes   **Cook** = 12 minutes   **Yield** = 4 to 6 servings

5 INGREDIENTS OR LESS

15 MINUTES OR LESS

Gnocchi with Creamy Pesto and Gorgonzola

Who said a super-rich sauce can't be made in 15 minutes? Grape tomatoes give this one a fresh and light counterpoint.

12   ounces (340 g) refrigerated or frozen gnocchi
1   cup (250 g) refrigerated or jarred Alfredo sauce
¼   cup (65 g) refrigerated or jarred basil pesto
½   pint (150 g) grape tomatoes, halved lengthwise
⅓   cup (40 g) crumbled Gorgonzola cheese

Cook the gnocchi according to the package directions. Meanwhile, combine the Alfredo sauce and pesto in a medium saucepan over medium-low heat. Cook until just heated through, about 2 minutes. Stir in the halved grape tomatoes.

Drain the gnocchi and toss with the sauce. Divide among pasta plates and top with the Gorgonzola.

Prep = 2 minutes   **Cook** = 13 minutes   **Yield** = 4 servings

Agnolotti with Spinach Sauce

These small half-moon shapes of pasta stuffed with cheese or chicken are in the refrigerated or frozen pasta section of your grocery store. Or, use small ravioli instead.

- 1 package (20 ounces, or 560 g) refrigerated cheese or chicken agnolotti
- 2 tablespoons (28 ml) olive oil
- 1 cup (130 g) prechopped onion
- 1 tablespoon (10 g) preminced oil-packed garlic
- 1 pound (455 g) prewashed spinach leaves
  Salt and pepper
- 1¼ cups (312 g) refrigerated or jarred Alfredo sauce
- ⅛ teaspoon ground nutmeg
- ½ pint (150 g) grape tomatoes, halved

Cook the pasta according to the package directions.

Meanwhile, heat 1 tablespoon (14 ml) of the oil in a large, deep skillet over medium-high heat. Add the onions and cook until golden, about 4 minutes. Add 1 teaspoon of the garlic and cook 1 minute. Add the spinach and nutmeg and cook until wilted, 3 to 4 minutes. Season lightly with salt and pepper, then scrape the mixture into a food processor or blender. Add the Alfredo sauce and puree until smooth. Return the mixture to the skillet and keep warm over low heat.

Heat the remaining 1 tablespoon (14 ml) oil in a small skillet over medium heat. Add the remaining 2 teaspoons garlic and cook 1 minute. Add the grape tomatoes and heat through, 1 to 2 minutes. Season lightly with salt and pepper.

Drain the pasta and toss gently with about ½ cup of the sauce. Divide among pasta plates and top with the remaining sauce.

Prep = 3 minutes   **Cook** = 12 minutes   **Yield** = 4 to 6 servings

Polenta with Saffron Chickpea Sauce

Look for tubes of polenta in the refrigerated produce aisle near the tubs of tofu. If you can find polenta flavored with sun-dried tomato and garlic, that works best here. Traditional flavor also works fine. As with most pasta dishes, grated Parmesan makes a wonderful garnish for polenta.

3	tablespoons (42 ml) olive oil
6	strips (1 1/2 ounces, or 43 g) precooked bacon
1 1/2	cups (195 g) prechopped onion
4	ounces (115 g) presliced cremini or white mushrooms
1	tablespoon (10 g) preminced oil-packed garlic
1/2	teaspoon dried thyme
1/8	teaspoon crushed saffron threads
1/8 to 1/4	teaspoon crushed red pepper flakes
1/4	cup (60 ml) dry white wine or sherry
3/4	cup (170 g) cooked or canned chickpeas, drained
1 1/4	cups (312 g) refrigerated or jarred tomato marinara sauce
1	pound (455 g) prepared polenta, sliced into 1/2-inch-thick rounds

Prep = 2 minutes   **Cook** = 20 minutes   **Yield** = 4 servings

Heat 1 tablespoon (14 ml) of the oil in a large skillet over medium heat. Add the bacon and cook until sizzling, about 2 minutes. Remove to a paper-towel-lined plate.

Add another tablespoon (14 ml) of the oil and increase the heat to medium-high. Add the onions and cook until golden, about 4 minutes. Add the mushrooms, garlic, thyme, saffron, and red pepper flakes. Cook until the mushrooms begin to release their liquid, 3 to 5 minutes. Add the wine or sherry and cook, scraping the pan bottom, until the liquid is nearly evaporated, 3 to 4 minutes. Add the chickpeas and marinara and reduce the heat to medium-low. Cook until the flavors have blended, about 5 minutes.

Meanwhile, preheat the broiler. Put the polenta on a baking sheet and rub all over with the remaining 1 tablespoon (14 ml) olive oil. Broil about 4 inches (10 cm) from the heat until lightly browned on both sides, 3 to 5 minutes per side, turning with a spatula.

Divide the polenta rounds among pasta plates and spoon the sauce over the top. Crumble the bacon over each serving.

Tortellini in Chunky Vegetable Sauce

Most supermarkets carry refrigerated tortellini, which tends to taste better than frozen or dried. In a pinch, frozen tortellini works fine. For extra zip, sprinkle on crushed red pepper flakes at the table.

- 3   tablespoons (42 ml) olive oil, preferably extra-virgin
- 8   ounces (225 g) zucchini, cut into bite-size chunks (2 cups)
- 2   cups (8 ounces, or 225 g) prechopped onion
- 2   cups (8 ounces, or 225 g) prechopped tricolor bell pepper
- 1   package (20 ounces, or 560 g) refrigerated cheese or vegetable tortellini
- 1   cup (250 g) refrigerated or jarred tomato sauce with chunky garden vegetables
- ½   cup (50 g) pregrated Parmesan-Romano-Asiago cheese

Heat the oil in a large skillet set over high heat. Add the zucchini, onion, and bell pepper. Cook, stirring frequently, until browned, about 8 minutes. Reduce the heat slightly if the vegetables are browning too quickly.

Meanwhile, cook the tortellini according to the package directions. Reserve ¾ cup (175 ml) of the cooking water just before draining. Drain the tortellini and add to the skillet. Reduce the heat to medium-low. Add about ¼ cup (60 ml) of the reserved water, scraping to remove browned bits on the pan bottom. Add the sauce and simmer until hot, about 2 minutes. Stir in the cheese. Add more of the reserved water, if needed, to loosen the sauce.

Prep = 6 minutes   **Cook** = 14 minutes   **Yield** = 4 to 6 servings

Pierogi in Tomato Vodka, Horseradish, and Dill Sauce

The plump Polish dumplings called pierogi make for quick weeknight meals. Pass extra horseradish at the table for those who like more kick in their food.

2 tablespoons (28 g) butter
1 cup (130 g) prechopped onion
1½ cups (375 g) refrigerated or jarred tomato sauce with vodka
¼ cup (8 g) minced fresh dill
2 tablespoons (30 g) jarred prepared horseradish
2 pounds (1 kg) fresh or frozen cheese-and-potato pierogi (24 pierogi)
Ground black pepper

Melt the butter in a large skillet set over medium heat. Add the onion. Cook, stirring, until golden, about 5 minutes. Add the sauce, dill, and horseradish. Set aside over low heat.

Meanwhile, cook the pierogi according to package directions. Drain and transfer to the skillet. Stir to coat evenly. Season to taste with pepper.

Prep = 2 minutes **Cook** = 10 minutes **Yield** = 4 to 6 servings

Ravioli with Roasted Red Pepper Cream Sauce

Alfredo sauce and pureed roasted red peppers make a dreamy sauce for ravioli. Use the frozen ravioli if you can't find refrigerated.

- 1 package (20 ounces, or 560 g) refrigerated meat or cheese ravioli
- 1 tablespoon (14 ml) olive oil
- ¾ cup (98 g) prechopped onion
- 2 teaspoons preminced oil-packed garlic
- 1 jar (12 ounces, or 355 ml) roasted red peppers, drained (about 1½ cups)
- ½ cup (120 ml) vegetable broth or water
- 1 cup (250 g) refrigerated or jarred sun-dried tomato Alfredo sauce
- ¼ cup (15 g) chopped fresh basil

Cook the pasta according to the package directions.

Meanwhile, heat the oil in a large skillet over medium heat. Add the onions and cook until golden, about 4 minutes. Add the garlic and cook 1 minute. Add the roasted red peppers and broth and reduce the heat to medium. Simmer for 2 minutes. Transfer to a food processor or blender and add the Alfredo sauce. Puree until smooth. Return to the skillet and keep warm over low heat.

Drain the pasta and toss gently with about ½ cup of sauce. Divide among pasta plates and top with the remaining sauce. Scatter on the basil.

Prep = 3 minutes   **Cook** = 12 minutes   **Yield** = 4 to 6 servings

Easy Lasagna

No-boil lasagna noodles and prepared tomato sauce make this lasagna a cinch. Lay the noodles crosswise and completely douse them with sauce or cheese.

1 pound (455 g) ground chuck
4 cups (32 ounces, or 905 g) refrigerated or jarred traditional tomato basil sauce
4 cups (32 ounces, or 905 g) ricotta cheese
2 cups (8 ounces, or 225 g) preshredded mozzarella cheese
1 cup (4 ounces, or 115 g) pregrated Parmesan cheese
2 large eggs
1 tablespoon (4 g) chopped fresh parsley
1 teaspoon salt
¼ teaspoon ground black pepper
12 no-boil lasagne noodles

Cook the beef in a large skillet over medium heat until browned, 5 minutes, breaking up the meat with a spoon. Drain off all but 1 tablespoon (14 ml) fat. Stir in the sauce and simmer over medium heat for 5 minutes.

Preheat the oven to 350°F (180°C, or gas mark 4).

In a large bowl, combine the ricotta, 1 cup (112 g) of the mozzarella, ¾ cup (87 g) of the Parmesan, the eggs, parsley, salt, and pepper. Spoon a layer of sauce over the bottom of a 13 x 9-inch (32.5 x 22.5-cm) baking dish. Arrange 3 noodles crosswise in pan over the sauce, leaving space around each. Spread one-third of the cheese mixture over the noodles. Spoon one-fourth of the sauce over the cheese. Repeat the layers of noodles, cheese, and sauce to make a total of 4 layers of noodles. Top the final layer of noodles with the remaining sauce, 1 cup (112 g) mozzarella, and ¼ cup (28 g) Parmesan. Cover with foil and bake for 30 minutes. Remove the foil and bake until lightly browned, about an additional 10 minutes. Let stand for 10 minutes.

Prep = 15 minutes   **Cook** = 50 minutes
plus 10 minutes standing time   **Yield** = 8 servings

Lasagna Bolognese

Making genuine Italian lasagna Bolognese takes many hours. With bottled sauces and refrigerated fresh wonton wrappers, however, the prep time is cut dramatically. If the pork mixture is cooled completely before layering, this can be refrigerated for up to 2 days before baking.

- 2 tablespoons (28 g) butter
- ½ cup (2 ounces, or 55 g) prechopped onion
- ½ cup (2 ounces, or 55 g) baby carrots, chopped
- 1 pound (455 g) lean ground pork
- 1½ cups (375 g) refrigerated or jarred tomato sauce with meat
- ¼ cup (15 g) minced fresh parsley
- ½ teaspoon ground black pepper
- 1 package (1 pound, or 455 g) wonton wrappers
- 1½ cups (375 g) refrigerated or jarred Alfredo sauce
- 1½ cups (170 g) preshredded Parmesan, Romano, and Asiago cheese

Preheat the oven to 350°F (180°C, or gas mark 4). Coat a 13 x 9-inch (32.5 x 22.5-cm) baking dish with oil spray. Set aside.

Melt the butter in a medium skillet over medium heat. Add the onion and carrot. Cook until sizzling, about 2 minutes. Add the pork and increase the heat to high. Cook, tossing, until no pink is visible, about 3 minutes. Add the tomato sauce, parsley, and pepper.

Spoon ¾ cup of the pork mixture into the prepared dish. Spread evenly (it will not cover the dish completely.) Cover with 3 wonton wrappers, cut to fit in a single layer. Spoon on ¾ cup of the pork mixture. Drizzle with ¼ cup (63 g) of the Alfredo sauce. Scatter on ¼ cup (30 g) of the cheese. Repeat the layering four more times. Cover with the remaining wrappers. Drizzle with the remaining ¼ cup (63 g) Alfredo sauce and the remaining ¼ cup (30 g) cheese. Bake until bubbling and golden, about 30 minutes. Let stand for 10 minutes before cutting.

Prep = 20 minutes   **Cook** = 30 minutes
plus 10 minutes standing time   **Yield** = 6 to 8 serving

Pastitsio

This classic Greek pasta casserole features both tomato sauce and cream sauce with flavorful additions of ground lamb, feta cheese, and a touch of cinnamon.

- 1 pound (455 g) penne or ziti
- 1 tablespoon (14 ml) olive oil
- 1½ cups (195 g) prechopped onion
- 1 pound (455 g) ground lamb
- 2 teaspoons preminced oil-packed garlic
- 1 teaspoon dried oregano
- ½ teaspoon ground cinnamon
- 1 jar (26 ounces, or 737 g) tomato sauce with garlic and onion
- 3 cups (750 g) refrigerated or jarred Alfredo sauce
- 1 cup (5 to 6 ounces, or 140 to 170 g) precrumbled feta cheese

Cook the pasta according to the package directions but just until slightly underdone.

Meanwhile, heat the oil in a large saucepan over medium-high heat. Add the onions and cook until golden, 4 minutes. Add the lamb and cook until no longer pink, 5 minutes, breaking up the meat. Stir in the garlic, oregano, and cinnamon and cook 1 minute. Stir in the tomato sauce and reduce the heat to medium-low. Simmer gently for 5 minutes.

Preheat the oven to 350°F (180°C, or gas mark 4).

Drain the pasta and mix half of the pasta with the tomato-lamb sauce in the saucepan. Mix the other half of the pasta with the Alfredo and feta in the pasta pot or in a medium-size bowl. Scrape the tomato-sauced pasta into a 13 x 9-inch (32.5 x 22.5-cm) baking dish. Scrape the Alfredo-sauced pasta over the top, spreading evenly.

Bake until golden and bubbly, about 30 minutes. Let stand 5 minutes before serving.

Prep = 3 minutes **Cook** = 35 minutes plus 5 minutes standing time **Yield** = 6 to 8 servings

Tuna Noodle Casserole

Prepared Alfredo sauce gives this
American staple a delicious new flavor.

- 8   ounces (225 g) wide egg noodles
- 4   tablespoons (56 g) butter, plus some for greasing
- ¼   cup (33 g) prechopped onion
- 8   ounces (225 g) presliced cremini or white mushrooms
- 1   teaspoon dried oregano, optional
- 3   cups (750 g) refrigerated or jarred Alfredo sauce
- ¼   cup (15 g) chopped fresh parsley
- ½   teaspoon ground black pepper
- 2   cans (6 ounces, or 170 g, each) water-packed
      solid white tuna, drained
- ½   cup (60 g) dry bread crumbs

Cook the pasta according to the package directions but just until slightly underdone.

Meanwhile, melt 2 tablespoons (28 g) of the butter over medium heat. Add the onions and cook until golden, 4 to 5 minutes. Add the mushrooms and oregano (if using) and cook until the mushrooms begin to release their liquid, about 4 minutes. Stir in the Alfredo sauce, parsley, and black pepper. Remove from the heat.

Preheat the oven to 375ºF (190ºC, or gas mark 5). Butter an 11 x 7-inch (27.5 x 17.5-cm) baking dish or other shallow 2-quart (2-L) dish.

Put the tuna in a large bowl, breaking it into coarse pieces. Drain the pasta and add to the bowl along with the Alfredo mixture. Mix well, then scrape the mixture into the prepared dish.

Put the remaining 2 tablespoons (28 g) butter in a small microwaveable bowl or skillet. Melt on medium heat for 1 to 2 minutes. Stir in the bread crumbs to moisten, then sprinkle over the top of the casserole. Bake until golden and bubbly, 25 to 30 minutes.

Prep = 5 minutes   **Cook** = 35 minutes (mostly unattended)
Yield = 4 to 6 servings

Easy Baked Macaroni and Cheese

If you use jarred sauce to make this, you'll need two 16-ounce (455-g) jars. For a cheddar-bacon variation, chop 4 slices thick bacon and sauté the bacon along with the onion. As long as you're at it, smoked cheddar makes a nice addition, enhancing the smokiness of the bacon.

12 ounces (340 g) elbow macaroni
¼ cup (56 g) butter, plus some for greasing
½ cup (65 g) prechopped onion
2½ cups (625 g) refrigerated or jarred cheddar cheese sauce
3 cups (12 ounces, or 345 g) preshredded cheddar cheese
2 slices white sandwich bread
⅛ teaspoon salt
⅛ teaspoon paprika

Cook the macaroni according to the package directions but just until slightly underdone.

Meanwhile, melt 2 tablespoons (28 g) of the butter in a large saucepan over medium heat. Add the onion and cook until golden, 4 to 5 minutes. Stir in the cheese sauce and 2½ cups (285 g) of the cheddar, and cook until the cheese melts, then remove from the heat.

Pulse the bread in a food processor until reduced to crumbs. Melt the remaining 2 tablespoons (28 g) butter in a small skillet over medium heat and stir in the bread crumbs and salt. Remove from the heat.

Preheat the oven to 375°F (190°C, or gas mark 5). Butter a 2½ to 3-quart (2.5 to 3-L) baking dish. Drain the macaroni and mix with the cheese sauce. Scrape into the prepared dish. Mix the remaining ½ cup (55 g) cheddar with the bread crumbs and scatter over the top. Sprinkle with the paprika and bake until golden and bubbly, about 30 minutes.

Prep = 5 minutes   **Cook** = 40 minutes (mostly unattended)
Yield = 6 servings

Tuna and Sun-Dried Tomato Pasta Bake

This update of the popular 1960's casserole has much more flavor thanks to the sun-dried tomato Alfredo sauce.

  8 ounces (225 g) medium to large shell pasta
  2 tablespoons (28 g) butter
  1 tablespoon (14 ml) vegetable oil
  ¾ cup (38 g) soft bread crumbs
     (1 slice bread, finely crumbled)
  ¾ cup (98 g) prechopped onion
  2 cans (12 ounces, or 340 g, each)
     tuna packed in water, drained
  1 cup (250 g) refrigerated or jarred
     sun-dried tomato Alfredo sauce
  1½ cups (195 g) frozen petite peas
  ½ cup (60 g) refrigerated or jarred
     roasted peppers or pimientos, slivered
  1 teaspoon ground black pepper

Cook the pasta according to the package directions but just until slightly underdone.

Preheat the oven to 350°F (180°C, or gas mark 4). Coat a 13 x 9-inch (32.5 x 22.5-cm) baking dish with oil spray. Set aside.

Heat the butter and oil in a medium skillet over medium heat until the butter melts. Remove 2 tablespoons (28 ml) to a small bowl. Add the bread crumbs to the bowl and toss. Set aside. Add the onion to the skillet. Cook, stirring frequently, until starting to brown, about 5 minutes. Transfer to the baking dish.

Drain the pasta and add to the dish along with the tuna, sauce, peas, peppers or pimientos, and black pepper. Toss to mix thoroughly. Cover with the reserved bread crumbs. Bake until golden and bubbling, about 35 minutes.

Prep = 15 minutes   **Cook** = 42 minutes
Yield = 4 to 6 servings

Baked Rigatoni with Sausage and Vodka Sauce

Baked pastas develop such wonderful flavors in the oven. Here, fennel seeds, sage, and sausage help along the savory flavors, while vodka sauce makes it creamy and fontina cheese adds a slight nuttiness.

1	pound (455 g) rigatoni or ziti
2	tablespoons (28 ml) olive oil, plus some for greasing
2	cups (260 g) prechopped red bell peppers
1 ½	cups (6 ounces, or 170 g) prechopped onion
1	pound (455 g) mild or spicy Italian sausages, casing removed
1	tablespoon (10 g) preminced oil-packed garlic
½	teaspoon dried sage
½	teaspoon fennel seeds
⅛ to ¼	teaspoon crushed red pepper flakes
1	jar (26 ounces, or 737 g) tomato vodka sauce with cream
2	cups (8 ounces, or 225 g) shredded fontina cheese
¼	cup (20 g) pregrated Parmesan cheese
3	tablespoons (7.5 g) chopped fresh basil
½	teaspoon ground black pepper

Prep = 10 minutes   **Cook** = 40 minutes (mostly unattended)   **Yield** = 6 to 8 servings

Cook the pasta according to the package directions but just until slightly underdone.

Heat the oil in a large saucepan over medium-high heat. Add the peppers and onions and cook until soft, 5 to 6 minutes. Slice the sausages in half lengthwise, then crosswise into ½-inch-thick half-moons. Add sausage to the pan and cook until well browned, 5 to 6 minutes, breaking up the meat with a spoon. Add the garlic, sage, fennel seeds, and red pepper flakes and cook 2 minutes. Reduce the heat to medium-low and stir in the vodka sauce. Heat through for 3 to 4 minutes.

Preheat the oven to 400°F (200°C, or gas mark 6). Oil a 13 x 9-inch (32.5 x 22.5-cm) baking dish.

Drain the pasta and add to the sausage-tomato sauce. Stir in 1 cup (112 g) of the fontina, 2 tablespoons (10 g) of the Parmesan, the basil, and pepper. Mix well. Scrape the mixture into the prepared baking dish and top with the remaining 1 cup (112 g) fontina and 2 tablespoons (10 g) Parmesan. Bake until bubbly and golden, 20 to 25 minutes.

Gemelli with Cucumbers and Smoked Salmon

Alfredo sauce mixed with cucumbers, scallions, dill, and smoked salmon create a delightful sauce.

12	ounces (340 g) gemelli, rotini, or other short-shape pasta
1	peeled, seeded, and chopped cucumber
1	teaspoon salt
3	tablespoons (42 ml) olive oil
1	finely chopped bunch scallions (white parts only)
2	teaspoons preminced oil-packed garlic
1	cup (235 ml) dry white wine
1½	cups (355 g) refrigerated or jarred Alfredo sauce
1	tablespoon (2 g) chopped fresh dill
4	ounces (115 g) smoked salmon
¼	teaspoon ground black pepper

Cook the pasta according to the package directions.

Meanwhile, toss the cucumber and ¾ teaspoon of the salt in a colander and let sit in the sink for 10 minutes. Rinse the cucumber and press out as much water as possible. Set aside.

Heat the oil in a large skillet over medium heat. Add the scallions and garlic and cook until soft, 2 to 3 minutes. Add the wine and boil over high heat until the liquid is reduced in volume by about one-third, 3 to 4 minutes. Reduce the heat to medium-low and stir in the Alfredo sauce and dill. Cook for 1 minute. Stir in remaining ¼ teaspoon salt, salmon, pepper, and reserved cucumber.

Drain the pasta and toss with the sauce.

Prep = 5 minutes   **Cook** = 10 minutes
Yield = 4 to 6 servings

Pizza, Tacos, and Sandwiches

Deep-Dish Stuffed Sausage Pizza

Prepared doughs make it easy to whip up pizzas and breads at a moment's notice. This one has a double crust filled with Italian sausage, sauce, and cheese.

- 1 pound (455 g) loose-pack Italian sausage
- 2 tubes (13 ounces, or 364 g, each) refrigerated Italian bread dough or frozen bread dough, thawed
- 1 egg beaten with 1 tablespoon (14 ml) water
- 1½ bags (12 ounces, or 340 g) preshredded mozzarella and provolone cheese, divided
- 1½ cups (375 g) refrigerated or jarred tomato sauce with sausage

Preheat the oven to 400°F (200°C, or gas mark 6). Coat a 14-inch (35-cm) round deep-dish pizza pan with vegetable oil spray. Put the sausage in a large cold skillet set over medium-high heat. Cook until no longer pink, about 8 minutes, breaking up the meat into small chunks.

Meanwhile, unroll 1 tube of dough and place in the pizza pan. Trim any overlapping dough pieces and press them into any bare spots to cover the bottom. Unroll the second tube of dough and spread it on a work surface. Trim the edges of the dough and press into any bare spots to form a rough circle.

Brush the dough in the pan with the egg mixture. Sprinkle on half of the cheese. Top with the cooked sausage, then drizzle on the sauce. Sprinkle with the remaining cheese. Cover with the dough circle and pinch the edges to seal. Brush with the egg mixture. Pierce the top crust several times with a small sharp knife.

Bake until golden and bubbling, about 20 minutes. Allow to sit for 10 minutes before slicing.

Prep = 10 minutes   **Cook** = 20 minutes
plus 10 minutes standing time   **Yield** = 4 to 6 servings

Mini Puff Pastry Vegetable Pizzas

Frozen puff pastry makes a fabulous—if untraditional—pizza dough. Here, the dough is cut with a biscuit cutter to create appetizer-size pizzas that elegantly puff up in just 15 minutes. Assemble the pizzas up to a month ahead of time, then pop them into oven before serving.

- 2 tablespoons (28 ml) olive oil
- 1½ cups (195 g) prechopped red bell peppers
- 4 ounces (115 g) presliced cremini or white mushrooms
- 2 teaspoons preminced oil-packed garlic
- ½ teaspoon dried oregano
- 1 pound (455 g) frozen puff pastry, thawed
- ⅓ cup (33 g) pregrated Parmesan cheese
- 1½ cups (375 g) refrigerated or jarred traditional tomato basil sauce
- 2 cups (8 ounces, or 225 g) preshredded mozzarella cheese

Preheat the oven to 400ºF (200ºC, or gas mark 6).

Heat 1 tablespoon (14 ml) of the oil in a medium skillet over medium-high heat. Add the bell peppers and cook 2 minutes. Add the mushrooms, garlic, and oregano, and cook until the mushrooms begin to release their liquid, 3 to 4 minutes. Remove from the heat.

Roll the puff pastry to ³⁄₁₆-inch thickness. Sprinkle with the Parmesan cheese. Spoon the tomato sauce over the cheese, then top with the mushroom-pepper mixture. Sprinkle on the mozzarella, then drizzle with the remaining 1 tablespoon (14 ml) olive oil.

Using a biscuit cutter, punch out 16 mini pizzas. (At this point, the pizzas may be wrapped in plastic and foil and frozen for up to 1 month.) Transfer to a baking sheet with a spatula and bake until bubbly and crisp, 10 to 12 minutes for thawed pizzas or 15 to 20 minutes for frozen mini pizzas.

Prep = 10 minutes **Cook** = 15 to 20 minutes
Yield = 6 to 8 servings (16 mini pizzas)

 5 INGREDIENTS OR LESS

 15 MINUTES OR LESS

Creamed Chipped Beef on Toast

Chipped beef is salted, smoked, dried beef. You can find it packed in jars in most grocery stores. Chipping the beef means pulling it apart in shreds like pulled pork. Simmering chipped beef with Alfredo sauce elevates it slightly above the old American classic.

- 2　tablespoons (28 g) butter
- ¼　cup (33 g) prechopped onion
- 4　ounces (115 g) chipped beef
- 2　cups (500 g) refrigerated or jarred Alfredo sauce
- 6　slices bread, toasted

Melt the butter in a large skillet over medium-high heat. Add the onions and beef and cook until lightly browned, about 5 minutes. Reduce the heat to medium-low and stir in the Alfredo sauce. Cook 2 minutes. Spoon over the toast on plates.

Prep = 0 minutes　**Cook** = 7 minutes
Yield = 6 servings

White Pizza with Spinach and Shrimp

Pizza made without red sauce can be a revelation. This one features the Italian colors—red, white, and green—with shrimp, ricotta, and spinach.

- 2 tablespoons (28 ml) olive oil
- 1 pound (455 g) peeled and deveined medium shrimp, thawed if frozen
- 1 tablespoon (10 g) preminced oil-packed garlic
- ⅛ teaspoon crushed red pepper flakes
- 6 ounces (170 g) washed spinach leaves
  Salt and ground black pepper
- 2 tubes (13 ounces, or 15 g, each) refrigerated Italian bread dough or frozen bread dough, thawed
- 1 cup (250 g) refrigerated or jarred Alfredo sauce
- ¾ cup (6 ounces, or 170 g) ricotta cheese

Preheat the oven to 400°F (200°C, or gas mark 6). Coat two 14-inch (35-cm) pizza pans or baking sheets with vegetable oil spray.

Heat 1 tablespoon (14 ml) of the oil in a large skillet over medium-high heat. Add the shrimp, garlic, red pepper flakes, and spinach. Cook until the shrimp are beginning to turn pink, the spinach is wilted, and most of the liquid has evaporated, 2 to 3 minutes. Lightly season with salt and ground black pepper and remove from the heat.

Meanwhile, unroll the pizza dough and press it into the pizza pans or baking sheets, trimming and pressing the dough, shaping it into rough 14-inch (35-cm) circles.

Combine the Alfredo and ricotta in a small bowl. Divide between the two dough rounds, spreading the mixture evenly. Top with the spinach and shrimp. Drizzle with the remaining 1 tablespoon (14 ml) oil. Bake until the crust is golden and bubbling, about 15 minutes.

Prep = 8 minutes **Cook** = 18 minutes
Yield = 4 to 6 servings

Grilled Pita Pizzas with Tomatoes and Gorgonzola

Pita bread makes a terrific base for pizza, especially when crisped on the grill. If you prefer to skip the grill, top the raw pitas as directed then bake at 450°F (230°C, or gas mark 8) until crisp and the cheese melts, 10 to 12 minutes.

- 1 pound loose-pack Italian sausage
- 6 pocketless pitas (6- to 8-inches, or 15- to 20-cm, diameter)
- 1 cup (260 g) Pesto Sauce (page 23) or commercially prepared pesto
- 2 tomatoes, finely chopped
- 1½ cups (180 g) finely crumbled Gorgonzola cheese (or another blue cheese, such as Maytag)

Put the sausage in a large cold skillet set over medium-high heat. Cook until no longer pink, about 8 minutes, breaking up the meat into small chunks.

Meanwhile, coat the pitas all over with cooking spray.

Heat the grill to medium. Brush and oil the grill grate, then put the pitas on the grill (in batches, if necessary) and brown the underside until nicely grill-marked, 1 to 2 minutes.

Remove to a work surface and invert so that the grilled side is up. Spread the pesto evenly over the grilled sides of the pitas. Scatter on the sausages, tomatoes, and cheese. Return to the grill with a spatula, put down the lid, and grill until the cheese melts and the bottom is browned, 3 to 5 minutes (watch carefully so that the pizza doesn't burn). Cut each pizza into 6 wedges.

Prep = 8 minutes   **Cook** = 10 minutes
Yield = 6 small pizzas (6 to 8 servings)

Provençal Spinach Pie

Savory vegetable pies are a staple all along the Mediterranean coast. This simple version can be dressed up with the addition of ¼ cup (150 g) each of raisins and pine nuts. Serve hot or at room temperature.

1	package (15 ounces, or 420 g) refrigerated pie crust (2 crusts)
1	cup (4 ounces, or 115 g) preshredded mozzarella-Asiago-roasted garlic cheese, divided
1	tablespoon (14 ml) olive oil
12	ounces (12 cups, or 340 g) prewashed baby spinach
1½	cups (375 g) refrigerated or jarred tomato sauce with four cheeses
3	tablespoons (48 g) refrigerated or jarred basil pesto
1	egg, beaten
	Ground black pepper

Preheat the oven to 375°F (190°C, or gas mark 5). Fit one crust into a 9-inch (22.5-cm) pie pan, allowing excess crust to flop over the sides. Scatter half of the cheese into the crust. Set aside.

Heat the oil in a large skillet over high heat. Add the spinach. Cook, tossing, until wilted, about 2 minutes. Set aside.

In a bowl, combine the tomato sauce, pesto, and egg. Stir to mix. Pour into the crust. Top with the spinach and the remaining cheese. Sprinkle generously with pepper. Top with the remaining crust. Fold the edges of the top crust under the bottom crust. Pinch to seal. Pierce the top crust several times with a sharp knife.

Bake until the crust is golden and the filling is bubbly, about 40 minutes. Allow to cool for at least 30 minutes before cutting.

Prep = 10 minutes **Cook** = 40 minutes plus 30 minutes cooling time **Yield** = 4 to 6 servings

Turkey Tacos

Here's a good basic taco filling that even kids will love. To make it spicier, use a mix of paprika and another ground chile such as ancho or chipotle. Or, use blended commercial chili powder but reduce the amount to 1 tablespoon (9 g).

12 (6-inch) corn tortillas
2 tablespoons (28 ml) olive oil
1½ cups (195 g) prechopped onion
1 cup (130 g) prechopped red bell peppers
1 tablespoon (10 g) preminced oil-packed garlic
1 tablespoon (7.5 g) canned or fresh chopped jalapeños
1½ tablespoons (10.5 g) sweet paprika
1 teaspoon ground cumin
1 teaspoon dried oregano
1 pound (455 g) ground turkey
1 cup refrigerated or jarred marinara tomato sauce
2 cups (40 g) preshredded lettuce
4 ounces (115 g) preshredded Monterey Jack cheese
1½ cups (338 g) refrigerated or jarred salsa or taco sauce

Preheat the oven or toaster oven to 350°F (180°C, or gas mark 4). Wrap the stack of tortillas and a few drops of water in foil. Bake until warm and pliable, about 10 minutes.

Meanwhile, heat the oil in a large skillet over medium-high heat. Add the onions and cook until golden, about 4 minutes. Add the bell peppers, garlic, jalapeños, paprika, cumin, and oregano. Cook 1 minute. Add the turkey and cook until browned, 5 minutes, breaking up the meat with a spoon. Stir in the marinara, reduce the heat to medium-low, and simmer gently until the flavors have blended, 5 to 8 minutes.

Put the lettuce, cheese, and salsa or taco sauce in bowls. Serve with the tortillas and turkey filling for layering the ingredients and folding over to make soft tacos.

Prep = 2 minutes **Cook** = 18 minutes **Yield** = 4 servings

Black Bean and Chorizo Tacos

Earthy, spicy, and a little smoky, these tacos make a terrific lunch. If you can't find chorizo, use another spicy fresh pork sausage such as Cajun andouille.

12 (6-inch) corn tortillas
4 ounces (115 g) fresh Mexican chorizo, casing removed
1½ cups (195 g) prechopped onion
1 tablespoon (10 g) preminced oil-packed garlic
4 ounces (115 g) presliced cremini or white mushrooms
1 tablespoon (9 g) ground ancho chile
1 teaspoon ground cumin
1 teaspoon dried oregano
1 can (14 ounces, or 392 g) black beans, rinsed and drained
1 cup (250 g) refrigerated or jarred marinara tomato sauce
4 ounces (115 g) precrumbled feta or goat cheese
1½ cups (338 g) refrigerated or jarred salsa or taco sauce

Preheat the oven or toaster oven to 350°F (180°C, or gas mark 4). Wrap the stack of tortillas and a few drops of water in foil. Bake until warm and pliable, about 10 minutes.

Meanwhile, cook the chorizo in a large skillet over medium heat until browned, 4 to 5 minutes, breaking up the meat into small chunks. Raise the heat to medium-high and add the onions. Cook until soft, 3 to 4 minutes. Add the garlic, mushrooms, ancho, cumin, and oregano. Cook until the mushrooms give up their liquid and the liquid has nearly evaporated, 2 to 3 minutes. Add the beans and marinara, then reduce the heat to medium-low and simmer gently until the flavors have blended, 5 to 8 minutes.

Put the cheese and salsa or taco sauce in bowls. Serve with the tortillas and filling for layering the ingredients and folding over to make soft tacos.

Prep = 5 minutes **Cook** = 15 minutes **Yield** = 4 servings

Tilapia Tacos

Fish tacos are popular snack fare in coastal regions of Mexico. Preparing them in your own kitchen is as easy as a day at the beach.

- 8 (6-inch) corn tortillas
- 1 cup (250 g) refrigerated or jarred tomato sauce with chunky vegetables
- 1 tablespoon (9 g) ground chili powder
- ¼ cup (60 ml) vegetable oil
  Flour
- 1 pound (455 g) tilapia fillets
- 2 bunches scallions, all parts, cut into 1-inch (2.5-cm) pieces
- 8 tablespoons (115 g) sour cream

Preheat the oven or toaster oven to 350ºF (180°C, or gas mark 4). Wrap the stack of tortillas and a few drops of water in foil. Bake until warm and pliable, about 10 minutes.

Meanwhile, in a microwaveable bowl, combine the sauce and chili powder. Cover and microwave on high power until hot, 1 to 2 minutes.

Heat about 2 tablespoons (28 ml) oil in a large skillet set over high heat. Dust the fish with flour, shaking off excess. Fry half of the fish until golden on the bottom, about 2 minutes. Flip the fish. Add half of the scallions to the pan in the space between the fillets. Lower the heat slightly if the fish is browning too quickly. Cook until the fish is opaque in the center and the scallions are wilted, about 3 minutes. Remove to a plate. Add about 2 tablespoons (28 ml) more oil to the pan. Repeat with the remaining fish and scallions, reserving about ½ cup (50 g) scallions to pass at the table. Fill the tortillas with fish, scallions, sauce, and sour cream, and fold over to make soft tacos.

Prep = 3 minutes   **Cook** = 12 minutes   **Yield** = 4 servings

5 INGREDIENTS OR LESS

15 MINUTES OR LESS

Open-Face Ham Sandwiches with Chipotle Cheddar Sauce

Deli beef or turkey—or a combination of beef, turkey, and ham—are also outrageously good in these spicy knife-and-fork sandwiches.

 6   slices hearty rye bread
12   thin slices sweet onion
12   ounces (340 g) shaved delicatessen ham
 1   cup (230 g) refrigerated or jarred cheddar cheese sauce
½ to 1   teaspoon ground chipotle chile

Lightly toast the bread and place the toast on a baking sheet. Top with the onion. Add the ham, one slice at a time, so the slices overlap onto themselves. Cover loosely with a sheet of aluminum foil. Cook in a toaster oven or preheated 350°F (180°C, or gas mark 4) oven until warm, about 8 minutes.

Meanwhile, in a microwaveable bowl, combine the sauce and ½ teaspoon chipotle. Taste and add up to ½ teaspoon more chipotle if you like. Stir to mix. Cover with waxed paper and microwave on high power for 1 minute, or until hot. Spoon over the sandwiches. Serve immediately.

Prep = 4 minutes   **Cook** = 8 minutes   **Yield** = 6 servings

 5 INGREDIENTS OR LESS

🕐 15 MINUTES OR LESS

Prosciutto Melts with Provolone

A round loaf of sourdough is perfect for these open-face sandwiches. If you can't find a rustic loaf, look for sturdy sourdough sandwich bread from Pepperidge Farm in the bread aisle of your super-market. To fill out the meal, serve with a pasta salad such as Creamy Rotini Salad with Broccoli and Tomatoes (page 126).

8	thick slices sourdough or other country-style bread
½	cup (130 g) refrigerated or jarred basil pesto
¾	cup (90 g) drained and sliced jarred roasted peppers
1	pound (455 g) (about 16 slices) prosciutto
8	ounces (225 g) (about 8 slices) provolone cheese

Preheat the oven or toaster oven to 400ºF (200°C, or gas mark 6) and move a rack to the top shelf.

Place the bread on a baking sheet and spread with the pesto. Top with the peppers, prosciutto, and provolone, dividing the ingredients evenly.

Bake on the top oven rack until the bread is toasted and the cheese is lightly browned, 5 to 8 minutes.

Prep = 4 minutes   **Cook** = 8 minutes   **Yield** = 4 servings

---

Italian Beef and Pepper Sandwiches

Braised beef actually improves in flavor if you prepare it several days in advance of serving. To reheat, slice the beef and reheat gently in the sauce in a large skillet on the stovetop. The directions below are for cooking the beef in the oven. If you prefer, use a slow cooker (Crock-Pot) and cook on low heat for 8 hours or high heat for 4 hours.

2½	cups (750 g) refrigerated or jarred tomato sauce with garlic and onion
1	green bell pepper, cut into slivers
1	onion, sliced
2	teaspoons Italian seasoning
2 to 2½	pounds (1 to 1.1 kg) beef top round roast
8	steak sandwich buns
12	slices (about 8 ounces, or 225 g) provolone cheese

Preheat the oven to 325°F (190°C, or gas mark 5).

In a large ovenproof pot, combine the sauce, bell pepper, onion, and seasoning. Stir to combine. Place the beef in the pot, spooning some of the sauce mixture over it. Cover the pot tightly with aluminum foil and the pot lid. Bake for about 3 hours, or until the beef is fork tender.

Remove the beef and place it on a cutting board. Cut into thin slices.

Slice the buns almost completely in half. Spread them open, cut side up, on a large aluminum-foil-lined baking sheet. Top the buns with beef, sauce, and cheese. Broil 6 inches (15 cm) from the heat until the cheese melts, about 2 minutes.

Prep = 5 minutes   **Cook** = 3 hours   **Yield** = 8 servings

---

Chicken Scaloppine Panini

Here's the translation: scaloppine means very thin cutlets of quick-cooking chicken; panini means little toasted sandwiches; and pesto, sun-dried tomatoes, and fontina cheese mean yum! The directions for using a skillet to cook the panini are below. You can also use a panini press or a George Foreman-style indoor grill with top and bottom grids. First, cook the chicken on the griddle or press. Then, cook the sandwiches on the griddle or press, lowering the top to gently compress the sandwiches. Both sides will cook at once.

- 3 tablespoons (56 g) butter
- 1 pound (455 g) presliced chicken scaloppine
- 8 slices sourdough or other country-style bread
- ½ cup (130 g) refrigerated or jarred basil pesto
- ½ cup (25 g) oil-packed sun-dried tomato strips
- 8 ounces (225 g) (about 8 thin slices) fontina cheese

Heat 2 tablespoons (28 g) of the butter in a large skillet over medium-high heat. Add the chicken (in batches, if necessary) and cook until browned on both sides, about 2 minutes per side. Remove to a plate.

Spread the bread with the pesto and top four slices of the bread with the sun-dried tomatoes, chicken, and cheese, dividing the ingredients evenly. Top with the remaining bread slices.

Melt another tablespoon (14 g) butter in the pan. Add the sandwiches (in batches, if necessary) and put a heavy weight on top of them, such as a cast-iron skillet or foil-covered bricks. Cook the sandwiches until golden brown and the cheese melts, about 2 minutes per side.

Prep = 5 minutes **Cook** = 10 minutes
Yield = 4 servings

Sloppy Joes

Despite the long ingredients list, there's
no chopping or prep work required.
The recipe calls for ground chuck
because its higher fat content keeps
the sloppy joe mixture moist and
flavorful. You can use lean ground beef
if you prefer. If you like a little heat, splash
on some Tabasco at the table.

1 tablespoon (14 ml) olive oil
1 cup (130 g) prechopped onion
1 cup (130 g) prechopped red bell peppers
4 ounces (115 g) presliced cremini or white mushrooms
2 teaspoons preminced oil-packed garlic
1 pound (455 g) ground chuck or lean ground beef
1 tablespoon (9 g) chili powder
1 teaspoon dried oregano
½ teaspoon ground cumin
½ teaspoon ground black pepper
¼ teaspoon salt
1 jar (26 ounces, or 737 g) traditional tomato basil sauce
¼ cup (13 g) oil-packed sun-dried tomato bits
1 tablespoon (14 ml) balsamic vinegar
1 teaspoon sugar
6 soft whole-wheat kaiser rolls or hamburger buns

Heat the oil in a large skillet over medium-high heat. Add the
onions and peppers and cook until the vegetables begin to
soften, 5 to 6 minutes. Add the mushrooms and garlic and
cook until the mushrooms begin to give up their liquid, 3 to 4
minutes. Scrape the vegetables to the side and crumble in
the beef. Add the chili powder, oregano, cumin, black pepper,
and salt. Cook until the beef is browned, about 5 minutes,
breaking up the meat with a spoon. Stir in the tomato sauce,
sun-dried tomatoes, vinegar, and sugar. Reduce the heat to
medium-low and cook until thick enough to sit on a bun without running, about 20 minutes. Serve on the buns.

Prep = 0 minutes   **Cook** = 35 minutes (mostly unattended)
Yield = 6 servings

Pesto Tuna Pitas

Cucumbers and lemon give these sandwiches a light, refreshing taste. If you have time, let refrigerate for 1 hour to allow the flavors to blend. The recipe calls for English cucumber (the long, skinny variety often wrapped in plastic) because this variety tends to have fewer seeds, thinner skin, and a less-bitter taste. If using garden variety cucumbers (Kirby cucumbers), peel and seed them before chopping.

2   cans (6 ounces, or 170 g, each) water-packed solid white tuna, drained
⅓   cup (87 g) refrigerated or jarred basil pesto sauce
2   tablespoons (28 ml) olive oil
    Juice of ½ lemon
¾   cup (120 g) prechopped celery
¾   cup (75 g) chopped English cucumber
½   pint (150 g) grape tomatoes, halved
½   teaspoon salt
¼   teaspoon ground black pepper
2   (6- to 8-inch diameter) pita bread rounds, cut in half

In a medium bowl, combine the tuna, pesto, oil, lemon juice, celery, cucumbers, tomatoes, salt, and black pepper. Fill the cut pitas with the tuna mixture.

Prep = 10 minutes   **Cook** = 0 minutes   **Yield** = 4 servings

Ham and Cheese Calzones

Big, puffy half-moons of pizza dough stuffed with cheese promise good eats. The ham adds a salty counterpoint of flavor. If you can't find preshredded provolone, use chopped deli slices of provolone.

- 8 ounces (225 g) presliced smoked ham, finely chopped
- 1 cup (4 ounces, or 115 g) preshredded provolone cheese
- 2 cups (16 ounces, or 455 g) ricotta cheese
- ½ cup (2 ounces, or 55 g) pregrated Parmesan cheese
- 1 teaspoon dried oregano
- 2½ cups (750 g) refrigerated or jarred traditional tomato basil sauce
- 2 tubes (13 ounces, or 364 g, each) refrigerated Italian bread dough or frozen bread dough, thawed
- 1 egg beaten with 1 tablespoon (14 ml) water

Preheat the oven to 400°F (200°C, or gas mark 6). Coat two baking sheets with vegetable oil spray. In a large bowl, mix together the ham, provolone, ricotta, Parmesan, oregano, and ½ cup (125 g) of the tomato sauce.

Unroll the pizza dough and press it into the two baking sheets, trimming and pressing the dough, shaping it into rough 14-inch (35-cm) circles. Brush the rim of the dough with the egg mixture.

Mound half of the filling onto one side of each round of dough. Pull the dough over the filling and pinch the edges closed with your fingers. Brush the tops with the remaining egg mixture. Pierce the top of the crust several times with a small sharp knife.

Bake until golden, 15 to 20 minutes. Let cool for 5 minutes before cutting.

Meanwhile, heat the remaining tomato sauce in a microwaveable bowl or saucepan on medium heat for 2 to 5 minutes. Serve the calzones with the extra sauce for dipping.

Prep = 15 minutes   **Cook** = 15 minutes
Yield = 6 to 8 servings

Soups and Stews

Valencia Gazpacho

When locally grown tomatoes are out
of season, this version of the Spanish
fresh tomato soup will fool you into thinking
summer produce is at hand.

- 1 English cucumber (15 ounces, 420 g), cut into chunks
- 1½ cups (6 ounces, or 170 g) prechopped tricolor bell pepper
- 1 bunch scallions (⅓ cup, or 33 g), white and light green parts, sliced
- 2 cups (500 g) refrigerated or jarred tomato sauce with garlic and onion
- 2 cups (475 ml) well-chilled orange juice
- 1½ cups (355 ml) ice water
- 1 teaspoon hot pepper sauce
- ½ cup (30 g) chopped fresh cilantro

In a food processor fitted with the metal blade or in a blender, combine the cucumber, bell pepper, and scallions. Pulse until finely chopped but not pureed, 18 to 24 times. Transfer to a large bowl. Stir in the tomato sauce, orange juice, water, hot pepper sauce, and cilantro. Refrigerate for at least 30 minutes before serving.

Prep = 5 minutes **Cook** = 30 minutes chilling time
Yield = 4 to 6 servings

Mediterranean Vegetable Soup with Pesto

France has *soupe au pistou* (vegetable soup with pesto and, usually, beans). Italy has *minestrone* (vegetable soup with beans and pasta, and sometimes pesto). Here's an easy version of this Mediterranean favorite. Bread and a salad complete the meal.

2   tablespoons (28 ml) olive oil

1   cup (130 g) prechopped onion

1   cup (130 g) prechopped carrots

1   cup (120 g) prechopped celery

1   large potato, peeled and chopped

4 to 5   cups (940 ml to 1.2 L) vegetable broth or chicken broth

1   cup (250 g) refrigerated or jarred tomato sauce with chunky garden vegetables

1   medium zucchini, chopped

1   cup (225 g) cooked or canned small white beans or chickpeas

1   cup (150 g) ditalini, macaroni, or small shell pasta (or broken thin spaghetti)

⅓   cup (87 g) refrigerated or jarred basil pesto sauce

Heat the oil in a large saucepan over medium heat. Add the onions, carrots, and celery and cook until softened, about 5 minutes. Add the potato, 4 cups (940 ml) of the broth, and tomato sauce. Bring to a boil over high heat, then reduce the heat to medium-low and simmer until the potatoes are tender, 25 to 30 minutes. Add additional broth if the soup is too thick. Stir in the zucchini, beans, and pasta and simmer just until the pasta is tender, 7 to 9 minutes. Stir in the pesto.

Prep = 5 minutes   **Cook** = 40 minutes (mostly unattended)
Yield = 4 servings

Cream of Asparagus Soup

If clumps of wild chives grow on your lawn,
snip them with scissors and use them in
this recipe (as long as you don't spray noxious
chemicals on your lawn). For a purely white soup
with green flecks of snipped chives, use white
asparagus instead of green asparagus.

2   tablespoons (28 g) butter or olive oil
1½ cups (195 g) prechopped onions
2   teaspoons preminced oil-packed garlic
1½ pounds (680 g) asparagus (20 to 30 spears), ends
    trimmed, tips reserved, and cut into 2-inch (5-cm) pieces
4   cups (940 ml) chicken broth
½   cup (120 ml) dry white wine or more broth
1   cup (250 g) refrigerated or jarred Alfredo sauce
1   tablespoon (4 g) snipped fresh chives

Melt the butter or olive oil in a medium saucepan over
medium heat. Add the onions and cook until soft, 4 minutes.
Add the garlic and asparagus pieces (reserve the tips). Cook
for 1 minute. Add the broth and wine and bring to a boil over
high heat. Reduce the heat to medium-low and simmer until
the asparagus is tender, about 5 minutes. Puree with a stick
blender or in an upright blender or food processor (in batches, if necessary). Return the soup to the pan and stir in the
Alfredo sauce. Heat through, about 2 minutes. Serve garnished with the chives.

Prep = 7 minutes   **Cook** = 12 minutes
Yield = 4 servings

Butternut Squash Soup

Perfect for fall suppers, this soup is creamy, elegant, and refined. To peel butternut squash easily, prick the skin several times with a fork. Microwave on high power until the skin softens, about 2 minutes, then peel from top to bottom with a vegetable peeler or paring knife. Or, better yet, look for peeled squash in your supermarket. A bit of minced red bell pepper and parsley make nice garnishes for the center of this soup.

2	tablespoons (28 g) butter or olive oil
1	cup (130 g) prechopped onion
½	cup (65 g) prechopped carrots
2	teaspoons preminced oil-packed garlic
1	teaspoon dried sage
1	medium butternut squash, peeled, seeded and chopped
2 to 3	cups (475 to 705 ml) chicken broth or vegetable broth
1	cup (235 ml) dry white wine or more broth
1	cup (250 g) refrigerated or jarred Alfredo sauce

Melt the butter or olive oil in a large saucepan over medium heat. Add the onions, carrots, garlic, and sage and cook until the carrots are soft, about 5 minutes. Stir in the squash and 2 cups (475 ml) of the broth, and bring to a boil over high heat. Reduce heat to medium-low, cover, and simmer until the squash is tender, about 15 minutes. Puree until smooth with a stick blender or in an upright blender or food processor (in batches, if necessary). Return to the pan and stir in the Alfredo sauce. Heat through over medium-low heat, 2 to 3 minutes.

Prep = 10 minutes **Cook** = 25 minutes
Yield = 4 servings

Beer Cheese Soup with Broccoli

Thick and satisfying, this soup goes well with steak or burgers.

6	tablespoons (84 g) butter
1	cup (130 g) prechopped onion
¾	cup (98 g) prechopped carrot
¾	cup (90 g) prechopped celery
¼	cup (30 g) all-purpose flour
2 to 3	cups (475 to 705 ml) chicken broth or vegetable broth
1	cup (8 ounces, or 235 ml) beer, preferably ale
2	cups (1 pound, or 455 g) small broccoli florets
2	cups (8 ounces, or 225 g) preshredded sharp cheddar cheese
1	cup (230 g) refrigerated or jarred cheddar cheese sauce
1	cup (250 g) refrigerated or jarred Alfredo sauce
1	teaspoon Worcestershire sauce
1	teaspoon dry mustard

Melt 5 tablespoons (70 g) of the butter in a large saucepan over medium heat. Add the onions, carrots, and celery and cook until soft, about 5 minutes. Stir in the flour and cook for 4 minutes. Whisk in 2 cups (475 ml) of the broth and the beer. Bring to a boil, then reduce the heat to medium-low and simmer until thickened. Meanwhile, melt the remaining 1 tablespoon (14 g) butter in a large skillet over medium heat. Add the broccoli and cook, stirring now and then, 2 to 3 minutes. Pour in ¼ cup (60 ml) broth and cook until the broccoli is crisp-tender and the liquid has simmered away, 1 to 2 minutes. Remove from the heat.

Puree the soup until smooth in the saucepan with a stick blender, an upright blender or food processor (in batches, if necessary). Return the soup to the pan and bring to a simmer over medium-high heat. Reduce the heat to low and stir in the cheddar, the cheese sauce, Alfredo sauce, Worcestershire sauce, and mustard. Cook gently, stirring now and then, until the cheese melts, 3 to 4 minutes. Stir in the cooked broccoli florets and serve.

Prep = 3 minutes   **Cook** = 35 minutes (mostly unattended)
Yield = 4 servings

Mushroom Bisque

Beef stock, shellfish, and pureed cooked rice are the hallmarks of classic bisque. Here, the shellfish gives way to mushrooms, but the rice still thickens the soup and beef stock flavors it. Short-grain rice is higher in starch and gives the bisque a creamier texture. Long-grain rice works, too. If you can, use a mix of sliced wild mushrooms such as oyster and shitake along with the cremini for a more complex flavor. For ultra-creamy soup, force it through a fine-mesh sieve after pureeing and before adding the Alfredo and reserved mushrooms.

2	tablespoons (28 g) butter
1	cup (130 g) prechopped onions
½	cup (65 g) prechopped carrots
½	cup (60 g) prechopped celery
1	pound (455 g) presliced cremini mushrooms
⅓	cup (65 g) short-grain rice (such as arborio) or long-grain rice
2	sprigs fresh thyme or 1 teaspoon dried
1	bay leaf
3 to 4	cups (705 to 940 ml) chicken broth or vegetable broth
2	cups (475 ml) white wine
1	cup (235 ml) beef broth
¾	cup (188 g) refrigerated or jarred marinara tomato sauce
1	teaspoon paprika
½	teaspoon salt
1	cup (250 g) refrigerated or jarred Alfredo sauce

Prep = 5 minutes   **Cook** = 50 minutes
Yield = 4 servings

Melt the butter in a large saucepan over medium heat. Add the onions, carrots, and celery, and cook until soft, about 5 minutes. Add 12 ounces (340 g) of the mushrooms and cook until they begin to release their liquid, 3 to 4 minutes. Add the rice and cook 1 minute. Wrap the thyme and bay leaf in cheesecloth or a clean coffee filter and tie with kitchen string or a clean plastic (not paper) twist tie. Add to the pan along with 3 cups (705 ml) of the chicken broth, the wine, beef broth, tomato sauce, paprika, and salt. Bring to a boil over high heat, then reduce the heat to medium-low and simmer until the rice is tender, 30 to 35 minutes.

Remove the herb bundle and puree the soup with a stick blender or in an upright blender or food processor (in batches, if necessary). Return the soup to the pan and stir in the Alfredo sauce and remaining 4 ounces (115 g) mushrooms. Cook over medium-low heat until the mushrooms begin to soften, about 5 minutes. Add additional chicken broth if necessary to thin out the soup.

Chestnut Soup with Mushrooms and Bacon

Try this soup in the fall when chestnuts are in season. It makes a unique holiday first course. The easiest route is to buy prepeeled chestnuts, which are available frozen and canned. But you'll get more flavor by roasting about 5 cups (725 g) of Italian chestnuts at 400°F (200°C, or gas mark 6) for 15 minutes, then peeling and chopping them. Garnish the soup with snipped fresh chives.

3	tablespoons (42 g) butter
1½	cups (195 g) prehopped onion
1	cup (160 g) prechopped celery
2	cups (290 g) pre-peeled chestnuts, thawed if frozen
3½ to 4	cups (823 to 940 ml) chicken broth or vegetable broth
1	cup (250 g) refrigerated or jarred Alfredo sauce
4	ounces (115 g) presliced cremini mushrooms, chopped
3	strips (¾ ounce, or 20 g) precooked bacon, finely chopped

Melt 2 tablespoons (28 g) of the butter in a large saucepan over medium heat. Add the onions and celery and cook until soft, about 5 minutes. Add the chestnuts and 3½ cups (823 ml) of the broth. Bring to a boil over high heat, then reduce the heat to medium-low and simmer until the chestnuts are fork tender, 25 to 30 minutes. Puree until smooth with a stick blender or in an upright blender or food processor (in batches, if necessary). Return the soup to the pan and stir in the Alfredo sauce. Heat through over low heat, 2 to 3 minutes. Add additional broth if the soup is too thick.

Meanwhile, melt the remaining 1 tablespoon (14 g) butter in a medium skillet over medium heat. Add the bacon and cook until sizzling, 2 minutes. Add the mushrooms and cook until they give up their liquid and the pan goes dry, 3 to 4 minutes.

Ladle the soup into bowls and spoon some of the mushroom-bacon mixture over each serving.

Prep = 5 minutes   **Cook** = 35 minutes (mostly unattended)
Yield = 4 servings

Tortellini in Pesto Broth

If you're feeling sniffly, this steaming, brothy soup will help. It's like chicken noodle soup, but tortellini are the noodles. The soup is mostly broth, so use the best-quality broth you can find (preferably homemade). If you like, sauté some finely chopped chicken breast along with the vegetables.

1 tablespoon (14 ml) olive oil
½ cup (65 g) prechopped onion, finely chopped
½ cup (65 g) prechopped carrots, finely chopped
½ cup (80 g) prechopped celery, finely chopped
8 cups (2 L) chicken broth or vegetable broth
20 ounces (560 g) refrigerated or frozen cheese tortellini
⅓ cup (87 g) refrigerated or jarred basil pesto

Heat the oil in a large saucepan over medium heat. Add the onions, carrots, and celery, and cook until the vegetables are just tender, 4 to 5 minutes. Pour in the broth and bring to a boil over high heat. Add the tortellini and boil until they are heated through (they'll float to the top), 3 to 5 minutes. Stir in the pesto and ladle into shallow soup bowls.

Prep = 3 minutes **Cook** = 8 minutes
Yield = 4 to 6 servings

Scallop and Corn Chowder

For an even fancier version of this company-worthy dish, replace half of the scallops with peeled raw medium shrimp. Sprinkle cooked crumbled bacon over each serving.

- 3 cups (390 g) frozen corn kernels
- ½ cup (50 g) chopped scallions
- 1 tablespoon (14 g) butter
- 1 teaspoon poultry seasoning
- ¼ teaspoon ground red pepper
- 2 cups (500 g) refrigerated or jarred Alfredo sauce
- 2 cups (475 ml) fish or vegetable broth
- 1 pound (455 g) bay scallops
- ¼ cup (15 g) chopped parsley

In a large pot set over medium heat, combine the corn, scallions, butter, poultry seasoning, and pepper. Cook, stirring occasionally, until fragrant, about 4 minutes. Add the sauce and broth. Increase the heat to high. Cook, stirring occasionally, until hot, about 2 minutes. Add the scallops and parsley. Cook until the scallops are opaque, about 3 minutes.

Prep = 5 minutes **Cook** = 10 minutes **Yield** = 4 to 6 servings

Catalan
Seafood Stew

Inspired by the maritime concoctions
of the Spanish Mediterranean coast, this
stew comes together quickly using prepared
vegetables and tomato sauce. It can even be
assembled in stages, making it ideal for
entertaining. Prepare the soup base hours or
even days ahead, then reheat gently, adding the
seafood just before serving. Use a medium- to
large-flake fish such as cod, halibut, or mahimahi.
Even catfish will work if that's all you can find.

    2   tablespoons (28 ml) olive oil
    ¾   cup (3 ounces, or 85 g) prechopped onion
    ¾   cup (3 ounces, or 85 g) prechopped tricolor bell pepper
    ½   cup (2 ounces, or 55 g) prechopped celery
    1   tablespoon (10 g) preminced oil-packed garlic
    ½   cup (120 ml) dry white wine
    2   cups (500 g) refrigerated or jarred tomato sauce with
        chunky garden vegetables
    2   cups (475 ml) water
   24   littleneck clams
    1   pound (455 g) mild white-fleshed fish fillets,
        cut into ½-inch chunks
   16   peeled medium shrimp (4 ounces, or 115 g)
    ½   cup (50 g) sliced green olives
    ¼   cup (15 g) chopped fresh parsley
    ½   teaspoon red pepper flakes

Heat the oil in a large pot over medium-high heat. Add the
onion, bell pepper, celery, and garlic. Cook, stirring occasionally, until soft, about 5 minutes. Add the wine and cook until the
liquid is almost gone, about 4 minutes. Add the sauce, water,
and clams. Bring to a rapid simmer. Cook until the clams start
to open, about 4 minutes. Add the fish and shrimp. Reduce
the heat so the mixture simmers gently. Cover and cook, stirring occasionally, until the fish and shrimp are opaque and the
clams open, about 8 minutes. Discard any clams that don't
open. Stir in the olives, parsley, and red pepper.

Prep = 5 minutes   **Cook** = 20 minutes
Yield = 4 to 6 servings

Mexican Chicken Tortilla Soup

If you've roasted a chicken and have leftovers, use the meat here along with those broken tortilla chips from the bottom of the bag. Or, buy a small rotisserie chicken, discard the skin and bones, and shred the meat. If you like, add chopped fresh cilantro to the garnishes given below.

2 tablespoons (28 ml) olive oil
2 cups (260 g) prechopped onion
1 tablespoon (10 g) preminced oil-packed garlic
1 tablespoon (9 g) ground ancho chile
4 cups (about 6 ounces, or 170 g) broken tortilla chips
6 cups (1.4 L) chicken broth
1½ cups (375 g) refrigerated or jarred tomato marinara sauce
2 cups (450 g) shredded cooked chicken
1½ cups (6 ounces, or 170 g) preshredded Monterey Jack cheese
1 ripe avocado, peeled, pitted, and finely chopped
1 lime, cut into small wedges

Heat the oil in a large saucepan over medium-high heat. Add the onions and cook until golden, about 4 minutes. Add the garlic and ancho chile and cook 1 minute. Add 2 cups (85 g) of the tortilla chips, the broth, and tomato sauce. Bring to a boil over high heat, then reduce the heat to medium-low and simmer until the tortillas are very soft, 15 to 20 minutes.

Puree with a stick blender or in an upright blender or food processor (in batches, if necessary). Return the soup to the pan over medium heat. Add the chicken and heat through, 2 minutes.

Divide the soup among bowls and top with the remaining tortilla chips, cheese, and avocado. Serve with the lime wedges for squeezing.

Prep = 7 minutes   **Cook** = 25 minutes   **Yield** = 4 to 6 servings

Chicken and Peanut Soup

Popular in the Caribbean and southern United States, peanuts are so much more than snack food. Here, they help form the creamy basis of a satisfying soup. If you're pressed for time and don't have any leftover chicken, buy a small rotisserie chicken, discard the skin and bones, and cut the meat into cubes. Garnish the soup with chopped scallions and crushed roasted peanuts.

2	tablespoons (28 ml) peanut oil or vegetable oil
1½	cups (195 g) prechopped onion
1	cup (160 g) prechopped celery
½	cup (65 g) prechopped red bell pepper
3 to 4	cups (705 to 940 ml) chicken broth
1	cup (250 g) refrigerated or jarred tomato vodka sauce with cream
1	cup (260 g) peanut butter
¼ to ½	teaspoon ground cayenne pepper
2	cups (220 g) cubed cooked chicken

Heat the oil in a large saucepan over medium heat. Add the onions, celery, and bell pepper, and cook until soft, 5 to 7 minutes. Add 3 cups (705 ml) of the broth and the tomato vodka sauce. Bring to a simmer, then reduce the heat to medium-low and simmer gently until the flavors blend, about 5 minutes. Puree with a stick blender or in an upright blender or food processor (in batches, if necessary). Return the soup to the pan and stir in the peanut butter, cayenne, and chicken. Heat through, 2 to 3 minutes. Stir in additional broth if necessary to thin the soup.

Prep = 2 minutes   **Cook** = 13 minutes   **Yield** = 4 servings

Turkey and Hominy Stew

Here's a Southwestern version of the classic southern Brunswick stew, using turkey, peppers, and hominy instead of the usual chicken, lima beans, and corn. Hominy is dried corn kernels that are treated with an alkali, such as lye, to remove the hull. It's available in the canned vegetables aisle of most grocery stores.

2	tablespoons (28 ml) olive oil
2½	cups (325 g) prechopped onion
1½	cups (195 g) prechopped green bell pepper
1	tablespoon (10 g) preminced oil-packed garlic
1	tablespoon (6 g) ground ancho chile
1	teaspoon dried thyme
4	pounds (2 kg) bone-in skinless turkey parts(preferably thighs)
2	cups (500 g) refrigerated or jarred tomato marinara sauce
2 to 3	cups (475 to 705 ml) turkey broth or chicken broth
1	can (26 ounces, or 737 g) hominy, drained
3	tablespoons (42 ml) Worcestershire sauce

Heat the oil in a large Dutch oven or heavy saucepan over medium heat. Add the onions and peppers. Cook until soft, 4 to 6 minutes. Add the garlic, ancho chile, and thyme and cook 1 minute. Add the turkey, tomato sauce, 2 cups (475 ml) of the broth, the hominy, and Worcestershire sauce. Bring to a boil over high heat, then reduce the heat to medium-low, cover and simmer until the turkey is cooked through and no longer pink, about 30 minutes. Add more broth if necessary to keep the meat covered.

Remove the turkey to a cutting board and pull the meat from the bones, using a fork or your fingers (the meat should shred apart easily). Discard the bones and return the shredded meat to the pot. Heat through, 1 minute.

Prep = 8 minutes   **Cook** = 40 minutes
Yield = 6 servings

Lamb Stew with Eggplant and Zucchini

1½ pounds (680 g) cubed boneless leg of lamb
1 teaspoon lemon pepper
1 tablespoon (14 ml) olive oil
3 cups (390 g) prechopped onion
1 tablespoon (10 g) preminced oil-packed garlic
2 to 3 cups (500 to 750 g) refrigerated or jarred tomato marinara
3 bay leaves
1 teaspoon crushed dried rosemary
1 medium boiling potato, chopped
2 medium zucchini, chopped
1 small eggplant, peeled and chopped

Preheat the oven to 350ºF (180ºC, or gas mark 4).

Season the lamb all over with the lemon pepper. Heat the oil in a Dutch oven or large ovenproof pot over medium-high heat. Add the lamb (in batches, if necessary, to prevent crowding) and cook until well-browned all over, 3 to 4 minutes. Transfer to a plate and cover to keep warm.

Add the onions to the pot and cook until golden, about 4 minutes. Add the garlic and cook 1 minute. Stir in 2 cups (500 g) of the tomato sauce, the bay leaves, and rosemary, and bring to a simmer. Scrape the sauce to the sides of the pot and return the lamb to the pot along with its juices. Layer the potato, zucchini, and eggplant over the lamb. Spoon the tomato sauce generously over the vegetables. Cover and roast in the oven until the lamb and vegetables are very tender, 2 to 2½ hours. If necessary, add additional tomato sauce to keep the liquid level about halfway up the meat and vegetables. Remove the bay leaves before serving.

Prep = 7 minutes   **Cook** = 2 to 2 ½ hours (mostly unattended)
Yield = 4 to 6 servings

Three-Chile Beef Chili

Dip into this warm and spicy chili like you slip into a favorite easy chair. It's that comforting!

- 2 tablespoons (28 ml) olive oil
- 2 cups (8 ounces, or 225 g) prechopped multicolored bell peppers
- 1½ cups (6 ounces, or 170 g) prechopped onion
- 2 jalapeño chiles, minced
- 1½ pounds (680 g) coarsely ground beef top round
- 1 tablespoon (9 g) chili powder
- 4½ cups (1.1 kg) refrigerated or jarred tomato sauce with meat
- 3½ cups (822 ml) beef broth or water
- 1 cup (60 g) chopped fresh cilantro
- ½ cup (120 g) sour cream

Heat the oil in a large pot over medium-high heat. Stir in the bell peppers, onion, and half of the jalapeños. Cover and cook, stirring occasionally, until golden, about 5 minutes. Scrape the vegetables to one side. Add the beef and chili powder. Cook, stirring occasionally, until the beef is no longer pink, about 5 minutes. Stir in the sauce and broth or water. Cook, partially covered, over medium-low heat until the flavors blend, about 10 minutes.

Pass the cilantro, sour cream, and remaining jalapeños at the table.

Prep = 5 minutes   **Cook** = 20 minutes
Yield = 4 to 6 servings

Classic Beef Stew

To make this stew in a slow-cooker, brown the seasoned beef in a skillet, then transfer to the slow-cooker. Sauté the onion, celery, carrots, and garlic and add to the slow-cooker along with remaining ingredients (including potatoes). Cook until the meat is fork-tender, on low for 8 hours or on high for 4 to 5 hours. Serve with crusty bread.

2	pounds (1 kg) cubed beef chuck
	Salt and ground black pepper
1	teaspoon dried thyme
½	cup (60 g) unbleached all-purpose flour
2	tablespoons (28 ml) olive oil
1½	cups (195 g) prechopped onion
¾	cup (120 g) prechopped celery
2½	cups (325 g) small baby-cut carrots
1	teaspoon preminced oil-packed garlic
1½ to 2	cups (355 to 475 ml) beef broth or dry red wine (or a mixture)
1	cup (250 g) refrigerated or jarred tomato marinara sauce with red wine
1	tablespoon (14 ml) Worcestershire sauce
2	bay leaves
3	medium boiling potatoes, peeled and chopped

Prep = 8 minutes   **Cook** = 2 to 2 ½ hours (mostly unattended)
Yield = 6 to 8 servings

Lightly season the beef with salt and pepper and the thyme. Roll in the flour.

Heat the oil in a Dutch oven or large saucepan over medium-high heat. Add the beef (in batches, if necessary, to prevent crowding) and cook until browned all over, 4 to 5 minutes. Remove to a plate and cover to keep warm.

Discard all but 2 tablespoons (28 ml) fat in the pot. Add the onion and celery and cook until soft, about 5 minutes. Chop ½ cup (65 g) of the carrots and add to the pot along with the garlic. Cook 2 minutes. Return the meat to the pan and add 1½ cups (355 ml) of the broth or wine, the tomato sauce, Worcestershire, and bay leaves. Bring to a boil over high heat. Reduce the heat to medium-low, cover, and simmer gently until the meat is fork-tender, 1½ to 2 hours. Add the potatoes and remaining 2 cups (260 g) carrots. Add additional broth or wine as necessary to keep the liquid about halfway up the meat and vegetables. Cover and simmer gently until the vegetables are tender, about 40 minutes. Spoon off any excess fat from the surface of the stew. Remove the bay leaves before serving.

Moroccan Chickpea Stew

Harissa, a fiery chile condiment available in well-stocked supermarkets, is the genuine accompaniment for this hearty vegetarian main dish. But Asian chili-garlic sauce will work in a pinch. Serve over instant couscous to soak up the tasty sauce.

¼ cup (60 ml) olive oil
2 cups (8 ounces, or 225 g) bite-size chopped zucchini
1 cup (4 ounces, or 115 g) prechopped onion
1 cup (4 ounces, or 115 g) prechopped tricolor bell pepper
1 cup (6 ounces, or 170 g) baby carrots, cut in small chunks
2 teaspoons ground cumin
1 teaspoon ground coriander
2 cans (15 ounces, or 420 g, each) chickpeas, drained and rinsed
1½ cups (375 g) refrigerated or jarred tomato sauce with chunky garden vegetables
½ cup (120 ml) water
½ cup (30 g) chopped fresh cilantro
   Harissa or Asian chili-garlic sauce

Heat the oil in a large skillet set over medium-high heat. Add the zucchini, onion, bell pepper, carrots, cumin, and corian-der. Stir to coat with the oil. Cover and cook until golden, about 5 minutes. Reduce the heat if the mixture is browning too fast. Add the chickpeas, sauce, water, and cilantro. Stir and cook until heated, about 5 minutes. Serve with harissa or Asian garlic-chili sauce at the table.

Prep = 3 minutes   **Cook** = 8 minutes   **Yield** = 4 to 6 servings

Sides, Salads, and Little Dishes

Spinach-Stuffed Portobellos au Gratin

Big, meaty portobello mushroom caps make delicious boats for all sorts of fillings. These are baked in the oven, but you could also grill them on a preheated grill with the lid down.

- 8 large portobello mushroom caps, stems removed (1 pound, or 455 g total)
- 2 tablespoons (28 g) butter
- ¼ cup (33 g) prechopped onion, minced
- 12 ounces (340 g) bagged baby spinach leaves
- 1½ cups (375 g) refrigerated or jarred Alfredo sauce, divided
- ½ cup (4 ounces, or 115 g) pregrated Parmesan cheese
- ½ cup (60 g) plain dried bread crumbs
- ¼ teaspoon ground nutmeg
- ¼ teaspoon ground black pepper

Preheat the oven to 375°F (190°C, or gas mark 5). Coat a baking sheet with vegetable oil spray. Place the mushrooms, smooth-side down, on the baking sheet. Set aside.

In a large skillet, melt the butter over medium-low heat. Add the onion. Cook, stirring, until fragrant, about 1 minute. Add the spinach and increase the heat to high. Toss until wilted, about 2 minutes. Stir in 1¼ cups (315 g) sauce, cheese, bread crumbs, nutmeg, and pepper. Spoon the spinach mixture into the caps, spreading evenly to cover the surface. Spoon on the remaining ¼ cup (60 sauce). Bake until bubbling and golden, about 20 minutes.

Prep = 10 minutes   **Cook** = 20 minutes
plus 10 minutes standing time   **Yield** = 4 to 6 servings

Parmesan Cream Biscuits

For a crunchy topping, sprinkle a few
tablespoons grated Parmesan over the biscuits
before baking. Dried thyme or dill (about
1 teaspoon) make good flavor additions.

- 2½ cups (300 g) all-purpose flour
- 2½ teaspoons baking powder
- ½ teaspoon salt
- 1⅓ cups (333 g) refrigerated or jarred Alfredo sauce
- ⅓ cup (80 ml) milk

Preheat the oven to 450°F (230°C, or gas mark 8). Whisk
together 2¼ cups (270 g) of the flour, the baking powder, and
salt in a large bowl. Whisk together the Alfredo sauce and
milk and add to the bowl. Stir with a large spoon until the
dough is just moistened and barely holds together (it will
look lumpy). Flour a work surface and your hands with the
remaining ¼ cup (30 g) flour. Using your hands, press and
shape the dough into a ball in the bowl. Turn out onto the
floured work surface. Quickly and gently press and shape the
dough, patting into a circle about ½-inch thick. Dip a biscuit
cutter or drinking glass into the flour. Press the cutter
straight down and lift straight up to cut out biscuits. Avoid
twisting. Reflour the cutter between cuts. Gently press the
scraps together to make 1 or 2 more biscuits.

Put the biscuits on a baking sheet and bake until risen and
lightly browned on top, 10 to 12 minutes.

Prep = 10 minutes   **Cook** = 10 minutes   **Yield** = 8 biscuits

Roman Rice Salad

Cooks in the Eternal City cut through
summer's scorching heat with this
cooling main dish.

⅓   cup (87 g) refrigerated or jarred basil pesto
3   tablespoons (42 ml) olive oil, preferably extra-virgin
2   tablespoons (28 ml) red or white wine vinegar
1   teaspoon ground black pepper
4   cups (660 g) cold cooked white or brown rice
1   cup (4 ounces, or 115 g) diced fresh tomatoes
1   cup (130 g) frozen petite peas, rinsed
¾   cup (98 g) finely chopped sweet or red onion
¾   cup (3 ounces, or 85 g) preshredded provolone cheese
½   cup (80 g) prechopped celery, very finely chopped

In a large bowl, combine the pesto, oil, vinegar, and pepper.
Whisk to mix. Add the rice, tomatoes, peas, onion, cheese,
and celery. Toss to mix. Serve immediately or refrigerate for
up to 2 days.

Prep = 5 minutes   **Yield** = 4 to 6 servings

Creamy Mashed Potatoes

Cheesy mashed potatoes were never easier. To vary the flavor, add roasted garlic or a few saffron threads. Or replace ½ pound (225 g) of the potatoes with turnips and prepare as for the potatoes.

1½	pounds (680 g) yellow-flesh potatoes (4 to 6 medium), peeled and coarsely chopped
¾ to 1	cup (195 to 250 g) refrigerated or jarred Alfredo sauce
4	tablespoons (56 g) butter
	Salt and ground black pepper

Put the potatoes in a large saucepan and cover with cold water. Bring to a boil over high heat, then reduce the heat to medium and simmer until the potatoes are fork tender, 12 to 15 minutes.

Meanwhile, heat ¾ cup (195 g) of the Alfredo sauce and the butter in a microwave oven or small saucepan over medium-low heat until the butter melts, 1 to 3 minutes.

Drain the potatoes and mash in the pan with a potato masher or handheld beaters. Mash in the hot Alfredo-butter mixture. Add more Alfredo sauce if necessary to thin. Lightly season with salt and black pepper.

Prep = 8 minutes   **Cook** = 15 minutes
Yield = 4 to 6 servings

Roasted Potatoes with Pesto and Peas

When properly roasted, new potatoes need very little garnishing. But pesto and peas make them something special.

- 1½ pounds (680 g) small red potatoes, unpeeled, halved (or quartered if larger)
- 2 tablespoons (28 ml) olive oil
  Salt and ground black pepper
- 8 ounces (225 g) fresh or frozen petite peas
- ½ cup (130 g) refrigerated or jarred basil pesto sauce

Preheat the oven to 450ºF (230ºC, or gas mark 8).
Put the potatoes on a large rimmed baking sheet and drizzle with the oil. Generously season with salt and pepper. Shake the pan to evenly coat the potatoes. Position the potatoes so that the cut sides are down.

Roast, without turning, until the potatoes are almost fork-tender and deeply golden brown on the bottom, 15 to 20 minutes. Scrape with a metal spatula to loosen the potatoes from the pan. Scatter the peas into the pan and roast 2 to 3 minutes more. Put several dollops of the pesto in various places over the potatoes and peas. Scrape and stir with the spatula until evenly coated.

Prep = 5 minutes **Cook** = 20 minutes
Yield = 4 to 6 servings

 5 INGREDIENTS OR LESS

Roasted Beets Alfredo

Red beets and white Alfredo sauce create beautiful pink streaks in this simple side dish. If you have green beet tops to work with, sauté them in olive oil with a little garlic, red pepper flakes, salt, and pepper. Serve these greens as another side dish.

1½	pounds (680 g) fresh beets (about 6 medium)
	Salt and ground black pepper
	Grated zest of ½ orange
	Pinch of ground nutmeg (optional)
1¼	cups (312 g) refrigerated or jarred Alfredo sauce

Preheat the oven to 400°F (200°C, or gas mark 6).

Scrub the beets, then trim off the tops, leaving 1 inch (2.5 cm) of stem attached. Individually wrap the beets in a double layer of foil. Place the wrapped beets on a baking sheet and roast until fork-tender, 50 to 55 minutes. Let cool enough to handle, then unwrap and cut off the root ends and stem ends. Peel by rubbing off the skins. Slice the beets ¼-inch thick.

Reduce the oven temperature to 350°F (180°C, or gas mark 4). Arrange the beet slices in overlapping layers in four 3-ounce (85-g)ramekins or small baking dishes or in a 1-quart (1-L) casserole. Lightly season with the salt and pepper and scatter on the orange zest and nutmeg (if using). Pour the Alfredo sauce over the top. Bake until hot and bubbly, 8 to 10 minutes (longer for a single large dish).

Brussels Sprouts and Bacon au Gratin

Don't be tempted to leave out the wine, sherry, or wine vinegar in this recipe. Just 1 tablespoon can balance the bitterness of sub-par sprouts and the steam helps to soften them.

1½ pounds (680 g) brussels sprouts, trimmed and halved

3 tablespoons (42 ml) olive oil

Salt and ground black pepper

½ cup (40 g) chopped pancetta or slab bacon

1 tablespoon (14 ml) white wine, sherry, or white wine vinegar

2 cups (500 g) refrigerated or jarred Alfredo sauce

1 slice sandwich bread

Preheat the oven to 450°F (230°C, or gas mark 8).

Place the brussels sprouts on a large rimmed baking sheet and drizzle with 2 tablespoons (28 ml) of the oil. Lightly season with salt and black pepper. Shake the pan to evenly coat the sprouts. Position the sprouts cut sides down.

Roast, without turning, until the sprouts are almost fork-tender and deeply browned on the bottom, about 15 minutes. Scatter the pancetta or bacon into the pan and roast until sizzling and the sprouts are fork-tender, 8 to 10 minutes more. Drizzle the wine or vinegar into the pan and scrape with a metal spatula to loosen the sprouts from the pan. Shake the pan to coat the sides evenly.

Meanwhile, put the bread in a food processor and remove the feed tube cover. Process until reduced to crumbs and, with the motor running, drizzle in the remaining 1 tablespoon (14 ml) olive oil and lightly season with salt and pepper.

Reduce the oven temperature to 375°F (190°C, or gas mark 5). Scrape the pan contents into an 11 x 7-inch (27.5 x 17.5-cm) or other 1½-quart (1.5-L) baking dish. Pour the Alfredo sauce over top and scatter on the bread crumbs. Bake until hot and bubbly, 10 to 15 minutes.

Prep = 12 minutes   **Cook** = 40 minutes
Yield = 4 servings

Curried Vegetables with Cashew Cream Sauce

Despite the long ingredient list, this dish gets to the table in just 30 minutes. Plus, it's so filling, it could be a vegetarian main dish served with rice and naan or pita bread. Garnish with a few cashew pieces for crunch. Look for cashew butter near the peanut butter in your market or in a health foods store. If you can't find it, grind ½ cup (75 g) cashews in a food processor along with the ¼ cup (60 ml) water called for in the recipe.

12	ounces (340 g) boiling potatoes (about 3 medium), peeled and cut into ½-inch pieces
½	cup (112 g) cauliflower florets
½	cup (65 g) prechopped carrot
½	cup (100 g) fresh or frozen cut green beans (1-inch, or 2.5-cm, lengths)
½	cup (75 g) fresh or frozen peas
1	tablespoon (14 g) butter
½	cup (65 g) prechopped onion
2	teaspoons preminced oil-packed garlic
1	teaspoon refrigerated pregrated fresh ginger
1	teaspoon garam masala
⅛ to ¼	teaspoon cayenne pepper
1	cup (250 g) refrigerated or jarred Alfredo sauce
½	cup (125 g) refrigerated or jarred tomato sauce with garlic and onion
½	cup (130 g) cashew butter
¼ to ½	cup (60 to 120 ml) water

Prep = 5 minutes   **Cook** = 25 minutes   **Yield** = 4 to 6 servings

Place the potatoes in a steamer basket set over a pan of simmering water. Cover and steam over medium heat for 5 minutes. Add the cauliflower and carrots and steam another 5 minutes. Add the green beans and peas and steam until all the vegetables are just tender, about 2 minutes additional.

Meanwhile, melt the butter in a large, deep skillet or medium saucepan over medium heat. Add the onions and cook until soft, 3 to 4 minutes. Add the garlic, ginger, garam masala, and cayenne and cook 1 minute. Add the Alfredo sauce, tomato sauce, cashew butter, and ¼ cup (60 ml) of water, stirring until combined. Cook until the flavors have blended, 5 to 7 minutes. Add a few tablespoons of water if necessary to thin the sauce.

Add the vegetables to the sauce and heat through, 3 to 5 minutes.

Turkish Fried Cauliflower with Tomato-Mint Sauce

A plain tomato marinara sauce becomes intriguing with the addition of fresh mint and a bit of cinnamon.

Sauce:

- 1½ cups (375 g) refrigerated or jarred tomato marinara sauce
- 3 tablespoons (18 g) minced fresh mint
- ¼ teaspoon ground cinnamon
- ¼ teaspoon ground black pepper

Cauliflower:

- 3 bags (8 ounces, or 225 g, each) cauliflower florets
- ½ cup (120 ml) water
- ¼ cup (60 ml) olive oil, preferably extra-virgin
- 1 tablespoon (10 g) preminced oil-packed garlic
- ¼ teaspoon salt
- 2 tablespoons (7 g) plain dried bread crumbs
- ½ cup (50 g) grated kasseri cheese or Parmesan/Romano cheese blend

Prep = 5 minutes   **Cook** = 10 minutes   **Yield** = 4 to 6 servings

FOR THE SAUCE:
In a saucepan, combine the sauce, mint, cinnamon, and pepper. Cover and simmer over low heat until the flavors have blended, 6 to 8 minutes.

FOR THE CAULIFLOWER:
In a large skillet set over medium-high heat, combine the cauliflower, water, oil, garlic, and salt. Cover and cook, tossing occasionally, until the water evaporates, about 8 minutes. Uncover and add the bread crumbs. Cook, tossing, until browned and tender, about 2 minutes. Remove from the heat. Add the cheese and toss to coat. Serve with the sauce on the side.

Southwestern
Corn Pudding

This creamy side dish practically puts itself together. And it can be assembled and refrigerated in advance of baking. Pair it with roast chicken or pork chops.

1 cup   (230 g) refrigerated or jarred cheddar cheese sauce
   2   eggs
  ¾   teaspoon chili powder
  ¾   teaspoon ground cumin
   1   bag (1 pound, or 455 g) frozen corn kernels, thawed
  ½   cup (2 ounces, or 55 g) prechopped onion, minced

Preheat the oven to 350°F (180°C, or gas mark 4). Coat an 8 x 8-inch (20 x 20-cm) baking dish with vegetable oil spray. Set aside.

In a mixing bowl, combine the sauce, eggs, chili powder, and cumin. Beat with a fork until smooth. Add the corn and onion. Stir to combine. Pour into the prepared baking dish.

Bake until golden and set, about 45 minutes.

Prep = 5 minutes   **Cook** = 45 minutes   **Yield** = 6 servings

Fried Provolone with Spicy Dipping Sauce

Sauce:

- 1 tablespoon (14 ml) olive oil
- 1½ cups (6 ounces, or 170 g) prechopped onion
- 1 cup (250 g) refrigerated or jarred tomato sauce with garlic and onion
- ½ teaspoon red pepper flakes

Cheese:

- ¾ cup (90 g) flour
- 1 cup (235 ml) cold water
- 1½ cups (355 ml) vegetable oil
- 12 ounces (340 g) mild provolone cheese in a large chunk, cut into ½-inch-thick sticks
- 6 lemon wedges

FOR THE SAUCE: Heat the olive oil in a medium skillet over medium-high heat. Add the onion. Fry until browned and crisp, about 4 minutes. Reduce the heat to low. Stir in the sauce and pepper flakes. Simmer on low while preparing the cheese.

FOR THE CHEESE: Place the flour in a shallow bowl. Add the water, whisking constantly, until smooth. Add a few drops more water if needed until the mixture is the consistency of sour cream. Heat the vegetable oil in a large skillet over medium-high heat until hot enough for frying. Test by sticking the handle of a wooden spoon into the oil. The oil should bubble up around it.

    Dip the cheese sticks into the batter, shaking off the excess. Drop gently into the oil. Fry in two batches, if necessary, to avoid crowding the pan. Cook, flipping once, until golden, about 2 minutes. Remove to paper towels to drain. Serve immediately with the dipping sauce and lemon wedges.

Prep = 5 minutes   **Cook** = 10 minutes
Yield = 4 to 6 servings

Hot Shrimp Cocktail

Spicy and warm, this shrimp cocktail is anything but ordinary. To serve cold, chill the shrimp and sauce separately.

1	lemon, halved
¾	cup (175 ml) white wine
2	tablespoons (20 g) preminced oil-packed garlic
1	pound (455 g) large peeled and deveined tail-on shrimp, thawed if frozen
3	tablespoons (42 g) butter
1	cup (250 g) refrigerated or jarred tomato sauce with garlic and onion
¼	cup (60 g) tomato paste
2	tablespoons (30 g) prepared horseradish
1	teaspoon Worcesterchire sauce
¼ to ½	teaspoon cayenne pepper
3	tablespoons (12 g) chopped fresh parsley
	Salt

Prep = 8 minutes (plus 1 to 4 hours marinating time)
Cook = 18 minutes   **Yield** = 4 servings

Squeeze the juice from half of the lemon into a large resealable plastic bag. Add the wine, garlic, and shrimp, massaging the marinade into the shrimp. Seal the bag, pressing out the air, and refrigerate for 1 to 4 hours.

Pour the contents of the bag into a large, deep skillet. Add the butter and bring to a simmer over medium heat. Cover and simmer gently just until the shrimp turn bright pink, 3 to 5 minutes, shaking the pan now and then.

Using a slotted spoon, remove the shrimp to a plate and cover to keep warm. Add the tomato sauce, tomato paste, horseradish, Worcesterchire sauce and cayenne pepper to the pan. Bring to a boil over high heat. Reduce the heat to medium and simmer until thickened to the consistency of cocktail sauce, about 10 minutes. Stir in the parsley and season to taste with salt. Let cool slightly.

Divide the warm sauce among four margarita glasses, shallow wine glasses, tumblers, or shallow bowls. Hook the warm shrimp over the rims of the glasses or bowls. Cut the remaining lemon half into wedges and serve for squeezing.

Fontina and Taleggio Fonduta

Italians have their own version of fondue known as *fonduta*. With egg yolks, butter, cheese, and cream, it's incredibly rich. Truffle oil makes it exceptional. You can buy white truffle oil in gourmet shops such as D'Artagnan, many of which offer online shopping. Serve the fonduta over rice or as you would fondue with dippers such as toasted buttered bread cubes, roasted cipollini onions, blanched broccoli, and fresh grape or cherry tomatoes.

1	pound (455 g) Italian fontina cheese, finely chopped or thinly sliced
8	ounces (225 g) taleggio cheese, finely chopped
1	cup (235 ml) milk
1	cup (250 g) refrigerated or jarred Alfredo sauce
4	tablespoons (56 g) butter
6	egg yolks
1 to 2	tablespoons (14 to 28 ml) truffle oil (optional)
	Pinch of salt

Prep = 10 minutes   **Cook** = 18 minutes
Yield = 8 to 10 appetizer servings

Put the fontina, taleggio, milk, and Alfredo in the top of a double boiler. Cover and refrigerate at least 4 hours, or overnight.

Pour the liquids from the pan into a large saucepan. Heat over medium-low heat until gently bubbling, 5 minutes, then whisk in the butter. When completely melted, reduce the heat to low and whisk in the egg yolks. Heat over medium-low heat for 15 minutes, whisking now and then.

Meanwhile, set the double boiler over simmering water and heat until the cheese melts, 15 to 20 minutes, whisking frequently. When the cheese is melted and relatively smooth (don't worry if the residual cream in the pan doesn't completely blend with the cheese), pour into the Alfredo mixture and heat over medium-low heat, whisking constantly until the mixture is smooth, about 5 minutes. Whisk in the truffle oil (if using) and a pinch of salt. Pour into a preheated fondue pot and keep warm over very low heat. Dip the bread or the vegetables of your choice, stirring often. Consume within 2 hours.

Potato Gorgonzola Puffs with Spinach

Frozen puff pastry shells are available in the frozen bread section of most grocery stores. To make this fork-and-knife appetizer into a main dish, skip the puff pastry shells, thin the sauce with a little milk, and serve it over cooked fettuccine.

- 2 tablespoons (16 g) pine nuts, toasted and chopped
- 1 pound (455 g) small white- or red-skinned potatoes (about 6), peeled and finely chopped
- 4 frozen puff pastry shells
- 2 cups (500 g) refrigerated or jarred Alfredo sauce
- 3 tablespoons (45 g) prepared pesto
- 3 tablespoons (23 g) crumbled Gorgonzola or other blue cheese
- 1 cup (about 2 ounces, or 55 g) packed prewashed baby spinach leaves

  Salt and ground black pepper
- 1 tablespoon (2.5 g) chopped fresh basil (optional)

Prep = 10 minutes   **Cook** = 30 minutes
Yield = 4 generous appetizer servings

Preheat the oven to 400ºF (200°C, or gas mark 6). Place the pine nuts on a baking sheet and bake until fragrant and golden brown, 3 to 5 minutes, shaking the pan once or twice. Remove to a plate.

Meanwhile, put the potatoes in a medium saucepan and add water to cover. Bring to a boil over high heat, then reduce the heat to medium and boil until the potatoes are just fork-tender, 12 to 15 minutes. Drain the potatoes and set aside.

Put the pastry shells on the baking sheet with the tops up. Bake until puffed and golden, 20 to 25 minutes.

Rinse the pan used for the potatoes and return it to medium heat. Add the Alfredo and heat through, 2 minutes. Add the pesto, Gorgonzola, spinach, and potatoes. Cook until the spinach begins to wilt, 1 to 2 minutes. Season to taste with salt and pepper.

Place the hot pastry shells on small plates. Remove the tops with a fork. Spoon the filling evenly into each shell, allowing some to spill over the side and onto the plate. Garnish with the toasted pine nuts and fresh basil (if using).

Mediterranean Chicken in Puff Pastry Shells

Seasoned ground chicken makes a handy filling for frozen puff pastry shells. Garnish these simple appetizers with chopped fresh basil. Or, if you prefer, you can form the chicken into patties for tasty summertime burgers on the grill.

1 box (10 ounces, or 280 g) frozen puff pastry shells (6 shells)

12 ounces (340 g) ground chicken

4 tablespoons (64 g) refrigerated or jarred red pesto sauce, divided

2 scallions, white and light green parts, finely sliced

Salt and ground black pepper

Preheat the oven to 400°F (200°C, or gas mark 6). Place the shells on a baking sheet. Bake until puffed and starting to color, about 10 minutes.

Meanwhile, in a bowl, combine the chicken, 3 tablespoons (48 g) pesto and scallions. Remove the shells from the oven. With a fork, carefully remove the puff pastry tops and set aside. Spoon the chicken mixture, mounding slightly, into the shells. Cover with the reserved tops.

Reduce the oven temperature to 375°F (190°C, or gas mark 5). Bake for about 18 minutes or until the chicken is sizzling. Let stand for 5 minutes before serving.

Prep = 4 minutes   **Cook** = 28 minutes plus 5 minutes standing time   **Yield** = 6 servings

Spicy Cocktail Meatballs

This recipe is a bit more fussy than most in this book, but it's worth it. The sauce is smooth and spicy; the meatballs are light and luscious.

1	slice sandwich bread
¾	cup (175 ml) water
3	slices thick bacon, minced
¼	cup (33 g) prechopped onion, minced
1	tablespoon (10 g) preminced oil-packed garlic
12	ounces (340 g) ground pork
8	ounces (225 g) ground beef
2	large egg yolks
1	teaspoon ground ancho chile
¾	teaspoon salt
½	teaspoon dried oregano
¼	cup (15 g) finely chopped fresh cilantro or parsley
1	tablespoon (14 ml) olive oil
½ to 1	teaspoon ground chipotle chile
2	cups (500 g) refrigerated or jarred tomato sauce with red bell pepper (or with garlic and onion)

Pulse the bread to coarse crumbs in a food processor or finely chop with a knife (about ½ cup, or 60 g, crumbs). Transfer to the bowl of an electric mixer and stir in the water.

Cook the bacon in a large skillet over medium heat until sizzling, 3 to 4 minutes. Add the onions and 1 teaspoon of the garlic, and cook until the bacon is cooked but not crisp and the onion is soft, 3 to 4 minutes more. Using a slotted spoon,

Prep = 30 minutes   **Cook** = 45 minutes
Yield = 10 to 12 appetizer servings (about 40 small meatballs)

transfer the bacon mixture to the mixing bowl. Stir in the pork, beef, egg yolks, ground ancho, salt, oregano, and 3 tablespoons (12 g) of the cilantro or parsley. Beat with an electric mixer on high speed until light and fluffy, 6 to 8 minutes. Form into 1-inch (2.5-cm) balls between your palms or with two spoons dipped in cold water.

Heat the oil (along with any residual bacon fat) in the same skillet over medium heat. Add the meatballs in two batches and cook until browned all over, turning frequently, 15 to 20 minutes (160°F, or 75°C, on an instant read thermometer). Using a slotted spoon, remove to a large warmed serving platter and cover to keep warm.

Add the remaining 2 teaspoons garlic and the ground chipotle to the skillet. Cook over medium heat until fragrant, 1 minute. Add the tomato sauce and simmer, scraping the bottom of the pan, until reduced to the consistency of thin gravy, 5 to 8 minutes. Transfer to a food processor or blender and puree until smooth (or use a stick blender if possible). Return the sauce to the pan along with the meatballs, spooning the sauce evenly over the meatballs. Cover and simmer over medium-low heat until heated through, 3 to 5 minutes. Transfer the meatballs to the serving platter and pour the sauce over the top. Garnish with the remaining 1 tablespoon (4 g) cilantro or parsley. Serve with toothpicks.

Green Eggs and Ham

Kids will love this version of the Dr. Seuss favorite come to life. If at all possible, use freshly made pesto or refrigerated pesto. The green color of fresh pesto is much brighter than the color of jarred pesto, which tends to be more drab green than bright green. Serve with buttered toast and heated stewed tomatoes.

2   tablespoons (28 ml) olive oil
4   slices Canadian bacon or 1 boneless ham steak (about ½-inch thick) cut into 4 pieces
8   large eggs
⅓   cup (87 g) fresh, refrigerated or jarred basil pesto
    Ground black pepper

Heat the oil in a large skillet (preferably nonstick) over medium heat. Add the bacon or ham and cook until lightly browned on both sides, about 3 to 5 minutes per side. Remove to a platter or plates and cover to keep warm.

Meanwhile, beat together the eggs and pesto in a large bowl using a whisk or fork. Lightly season with black pepper.

Reduce the heat to low and pour the eggs into the skillet. Cook gently, scraping the pan bottom now and then with a plastic spatula or spoon, until the eggs form soft curds, about 10 minutes. Serve with the bacon or ham.

Prep = 3 minutes   **Cook** = 18 minutes   **Yield** = 4 modest servings

Ratatouille Frittata

In the South of France, the tomato-vegetable stew ratatouille is as common as ketchup. It's a marvelous companion for eggs.

2 tablespoons (28 ml) olive oil, divided
1 cup (4 ounces, or 115 g) bite-size zucchini chunks
1 cup (4 ounces, or 115 g) prechopped onion
1 cup (4 ounces, or 115 g) prechopped tricolor bell pepper
2 tablespoons (7.5 g) finely chopped fresh tarragon
8 eggs
⅓ cup (80 ml) water
¼ teaspoon ground black pepper
   Salt
1 cup (250 g) refrigerated or jarred tomato sauce with chunky garden vegetables
¾ cup (3 ounces, or 90 ml) shredded Swiss cheese

In a large skillet, preferably nonstick, heat 1 tablespoon (14 ml) oil over medium-high heat. Add the zucchini, onion, bell pepper, and tarragon. Stir. Cover and cook until golden, about 5 minutes. Remove to a plate and set aside.

Meanwhile, in a bowl, beat the eggs, water, pepper, and a pinch of salt. Return the skillet to medium-high heat. Add the remaining 1 tablespoon (14 ml) oil. When the oil is hot, pour in the egg mixture. Cook for 3 to 4 minutes, lifting the edges of the eggs with a spatula as they set to let uncooked egg run underneath. When the bottom is set, scatter the reserved vegetables over the top. Cover with the sauce and cheese. Cover and reduce the heat to low. Cook for 3 minutes or until the eggs are set and the cheese is melted. If desired, broil for 2 to 3 minutes, about 8 inches (20 cm) from the heat source, to brown the cheese.

Prep = 5 minutes   **Cook** = 15 minutes   **Yield** = 4 servings

Sun-Dried Tomato and Asparagus Quiche

This savory pie can be served warm or at room temperature as an appetizer or a main course for brunch. For a nice flavor addition, toss in some finely diced ham or prosciutto.

- 6 ounces (170 g) (1½ cups) asparagus, cut into ½-inch pieces
- 1 ready-made refrigerated 9-inch (22.5-cm) pie crust
- 1 cup (250 g) refrigerated or jarred sun-dried tomato Alfredo sauce
- 2 eggs
- ½ teaspoon dried tarragon
- ½ teaspoon ground black pepper

Preheat the oven to 350°F (180°C, or gas mark 4).

Heat about ½ cup (120 ml) of water in a medium skillet over high heat. Add the asparagus. Cover and cook until the asparagus is bright green, about 2 minutes. Drain. Rinse well with cold tap water. Pat dry and place in an even layer in the pie crust.

In a mixing bowl, combine the sauce, eggs, tarragon, and pepper. Beat with a fork until smooth. Pour into the crust. Bake until set, about 35 minutes. Let stand for 15 minutes before cutting.

Prep = 5 minutes **Cook** = 35 minutes
plus 15 minutes standing time **Yield** = 4 to 6 servings

Potato, Pepper, and Spinach Strata

This layered casserole is the perfect brunch dish for spring or early fall. You can assemble the whole thing the night before, then pop it in the oven the next morning.

1 pound (455 g) Yukon Gold or other yellow-flesh potatoes, peeled and sliced ⅛-inch-thick

1 cup (130 g) prechopped red bell pepper

3 cups (705 ml) whole milk

1 cup (235 ml) vegetable broth or water

1 cup (130 g) prechopped onion

1 teaspoon dried thyme

Salt and ground black pepper

8 large eggs

2 cups (500 g) refrigerated or jarred Alfredo sauce

1 tablespoon (15 g) Dijon mustard

12 slices sourdough or firm white sandwich bread, lightly toasted

3 ounces (85 g) (about 2 cups) prewashed baby spinach leaves

2 cups (240 g) grated Gruyère cheese

Prep = 15 minutes   **Cook** = 60 minutes (mostly unattended)
Yield = 4 to 6 servings

Put the potatoes, bell pepper, 1 cup (235 ml) of the milk, the broth, onion, and thyme in a deep, wide skillet. Bring to a simmer over medium heat. Cover and simmer until the potatoes are almost tender, 12 to 15 minutes. Uncover and simmer until the potatoes are fork-tender and most of the liquid evaporates, 5 to 8 minutes. Season with salt and pepper ($\frac{1}{4}$ to $\frac{1}{2}$ teaspoon each).

Preheat the oven to 350°F (180°C, or gas mark 5). In a large bowl, whisk together the eggs, Alfredo sauce, mustard, and remaining 2 cups (475 ml) milk. Season with salt and pepper.

Line the bottom of a shallow 4-quart (3.8-L) baking dish (such as a 15- x 10-inch, or 37.5 x 25-cm, dish) with 6 of the bread slices. Pour just enough of the egg mixture over the bread to cover, spreading it out to coat the bread completely. Layer the spinach leaves evenly over top. Spread the potato filling evenly over the spinach. Sprinkle with half the cheese, then layer with the remaining 6 slices bread. Pour the remaining egg mixture over the top, pushing on the bread to thoroughly saturate it. Sprinkle the remaining cheese on top. (At this point, the dish can be covered and refrigerated overnight if needed. This also enriches the flavor.) Bake, uncovered, until the eggs are set and the cheese is lightly browned on top, 40 to 50 minutes.

Mushroom and Boursin Soufflé

Boursin is a garlic-and-herb flavored creamy cheese with a velvety, light texture. If you can't find boursin, use crumbled goat cheese. To make individual soufflés, replace the large soufflé dish with six 1½-cup straight-sided ramekins. Serve the soufflé as soon as it comes out of oven. After that, it will gradually deflate.

4	tablespoons (56 g) butter
1	tablespoon (3.5 g) plain dried bread crumbs
½	cup (65 g) prechopped onions, finely chopped
1	pound (455 g) presliced cremini or white mushrooms, chopped
1½	cups (375 g) refrigerated or jarred Alfredo sauce
6	large eggs, separated
1	package (5 ounces, or 140 g) Boursin cheese, finely crumbled (about 1 cup)
2	tablespoons (8 g) chopped fresh parsley
1	teaspoon Dijon mustard
	Salt and ground black pepper
	Pinch of cream of tartar

Prep = 12 minutes **Cook** = 40 minutes (mostly unattended)
Yield = 6 servings

Preheat the oven to 400ºF (200ºC, or gas mark 6). Generously butter a 2-quart (2-L) soufflé dish or deep baking dish with 1 to 2 teaspoons of the butter. Sprinkle with the bread crumbs and rotate the pan until all the crumbs have adhered.

Heat the remaining butter in the same saucepan over medium heat. Add the onion and cook until tender, about 4 minutes. Add the mushrooms and cook until they give up their liquid and most of the liquid evaporates, 5 to 6 minutes. Remove to a colander to drain.

Add the Alfredo sauce to the saucepan and heat through. Remove from the heat and stir in the egg yolks, cheese, parsley, and mustard. Lightly season with salt and pepper. Stir in the mushrooms.

Put the egg whites and cream of tartar in a clean large bowl. Beat with clean beaters on medium speed until stiff peaks form when the beaters are lifted, about 5 minutes. Stir about ½ cup of the egg whites into the mushroom mixture to lighten it. Gently fold in the remaining egg whites, being careful not to deflate the egg whites.

Gently scrape into the prepared dish and bake until puffed and browned on top, 30 to 35 minutes. A skewer inserted into the center should come out slightly moist but not wet.

 5 INGREDIENTS OR LESS

 15 MINUTES OR LESS

Chips and Hot Cheddar Dip

Perfect for football parties, this dip
can be kept warm on a stovetop. Or, set
the saucepan on a heating pad set to high.
Serve with vegetables such as lightly steamed
broccoli or sliced red bell peppers. Or, serve with
hunks of bread for dipping.

1½ cups (345 g) refrigerated or jarred cheddar
cheese sauce

2 cups (8 ounces, or 225 g) preshredded cheddar or
pepper Jack cheese

¾ cup (170 g) refrigerated or jarred tomato salsa, drained

1 teaspoon chili powder

1 large bag (20 ounces, or 560 g) tortilla chips

Combine the cheese sauce, cheddar or pepper Jack, drained
salsa, and chili powder in a medium saucepan. Heat over
medium-low heat until the cheese melts and the flavors have
blended, 10 to 12 minutes. Serve with the tortilla chips.

Prep = 2 minutes **Cook** = 12 minutes
Yield = 8 to 10 servings (4 cups, or 920 g)

Crostini with Tomato Hazelnut Spread

Thin homemade toasts always taste better than store-bought crackers. But, in a pinch, crackers can stand in for the crostini here. If you can't find hazelnuts, use blanched almonds instead.

- 1 baguette (8 ounces, or 225 g), sliced on the diagonal about ¼-inch thick (about 16 slices)
- 3 cloves garlic
- ⅔ cup (155 ml) olive oil
  Salt and ground black pepper
- ¾ cup (112 g) blanched hazelnuts
- 1¼ cups (312 g) refrigerated or jarred tomato sauce with garlic and onion
- 1 tablespoon (7 g) paprika
- 1 tablespoon (14 ml) balsamic vinegar
- 2 teaspoons lemon juice
- ⅛ teaspoon cayenne pepper

Preheat the oven to 400ºF (200ºC, or gas mark 6). Put the bread slices on a large baking sheet. Smash 2 of the garlic cloves and drop into a small bowl. Mix in ⅓ cup (78 ml) of the olive oil, stirring a few times.

Brush the garlic oil on both sides of the bread slices, then lightly season the slices with salt and pepper. Bake until golden on both sides, 4 to 6 minutes per side. Remove from the oven and let cool slightly.

Meanwhile, put the hazelnuts, tomato sauce, paprika, balsamic vinegar, lemon juice, and cayenne pepper in a food processor. Season with salt and pepper. Puree until the nuts are ground. With the machine running, add the remaining ⅓ cup (78 ml) olive oil through the feed tube. Process until the mixture forms a loose paste (resembling loose tomato paste), scraping down the sides as necessary. Serve with the crostini for dipping or spreading.

Prep = 10 minutes   **Cook** = 10 minutes
Yield = 8 servings

Pesto, Roasted Pepper, and Provolone Spirals

Here's a pretty appetizer for a casual party—especially in the summer. It requires no cooking and comes together in less than 15 minutes.

4 (10-inch) flour tortillas
½ cup (130 g) refrigerated or jarred basil pesto
8 ounces (225 g) (about 8 slices) presliced provolone cheese
2 cups (about 2 ounces, or 55 g) prewashed arugula or baby spinach leaves
1 cup (120 g) drained jarred roasted red pepper strips

Put two of the tortillas on a microwaveable plate. Heat very briefly in a microwave oven on medium heat until pliable and just slightly warm, 8 to 10 seconds. Repeat with the other two tortillas.

Spread the pesto evenly over the tortillas. Top with the provolone, arugula, and roasted peppers. Roll up tightly, then cut crosswise into slices about ½-inch thick.

Prep = 10 minutes   **Cook** = 20 seconds
Yield = 8 servings (28 to 32 spirals)

Deviled
Crab Bites

Looking for a fast, fancy appetizer? The
filling for these appetizers can be made a
day ahead and refrigerated. Then, simply fill the
phyllo shells (up to 1 hour ahead) and bake
10 minutes before serving.

- 1 tablespoon (14 g) butter
- 2 teaspoons preminced oil-packed garlic
- 2 tablespoons (28 ml) white wine or sherry or
  1 tablespoon (14 ml) lemon juice
- 4 ounces (115 g) (½ cup) cream cheese
- ¾ cup (188 g) refrigerated or jarred Alfredo sauce
- 1 teaspoon Dijon mustard
- ½ teaspoon salt
- ¼ teaspoon cayenne pepper
- 1 tablespoon (2 g) minced fresh tarragon, dill, or parsley
- 1 pound (455 g) jumbo lump crab meat
- 2 boxes (2.1 ounces, or 58.8 g, each) mini phyllo shells,
  thawed if frozen
- ⅔ cup (60 g) pregrated Parmesan cheese

Melt the butter in a medium saucepan over medium heat.
Add the garlic and cook until fragrant, 2 to 3 minutes. Add
the wine or lemon juice and simmer until the liquid is nearly
evaporated, 2 minutes. Add the cream cheese and Alfredo
sauce, mustard, salt, and cayenne and stir until the cheese
melts, 2 to 3 minutes. Remove from the heat and gently stir
in the tarragon and crab.

Preheat the oven to 350°F (180°C, or gas mark 4). Spoon
the crab mixture into the phyllo shells and sprinkle with the
Parmesan. Bake until heated through, 8 to 10 minutes.

Prep = 10 minutes   **Cook** = 18 minutes
Yield = 8 to 10 appetizer servings

Index

Acknowledgments

Two hundred twelve jars of sauce and 16 months later, it's time to thank everyone who helped bring this book into your hands. It has been a pleasure to work with such smart, inventive, and fun people. For tasting umpteen varieties of pasta sauce, testing recipes, and offering helpful comments, thanks to Cathy, Ken, Nick, Tomias, and Tessa Peoples; Mark Taylor; Mark Bowman; Jill, Mike, Bradley, and Scott Polek; Tom Aczel and Michele Raes; Dan McKinney; Sharon, Walter, Tess, and Emma Sanders; Andrew and Kim Brubaker; Doug Ashby and Danielle Lubené; and Billy Melcher.

Big thanks to Meera Malik for months of recipe testing, a keen eye, and for listening to loud music when it was needed most.

My deepest gratitude goes out to Lisa Ekus, Holly Schmidt, Rosalind Wanke, Claire MacMaster, John Gettings, Laura McFadden, Sylvia McArdle, and Derek Sussner for helping to make this book look, feel, and read the wonderful way it does.

A special thank-you to Sharon Sanders for her inimitable taste buds and assistance with recipe development early on in the writing. Thanks also to Andrew Schloss, Raghavan Iyer, and Nick Malgieri for encouragement, laughs, and down-to-earth insight. To Christine Bucher, hugs and kisses for that endless supply of wit, wisdom, and sauciness. And, lastly, to August and Maddox, thanks for eagerly licking those little fingers.

About the Author

David Joachim has authored, edited, or collaborated on more than 25 cookbooks. He is the author of the International Association of Culinary Professionals (IACP) award-winning reference book, *The Food Substitutions Bible*. He also wrote *A Man, A Can, A Plan*, which has more than 500,000 copies in print, and *A Man, A Can, A Grill*, a *New York Times* bestseller.

Joachim is former food editor of *Vegetarian Gourmet* magazine, and his writing and tips have appeared in numerous national magazines such as *Cook's Illustrated, Cooking Light, Cooking Pleasures, Relish, Prevention, Fitness, Men's Health*, and *Bicycling*. As an author and spokesperson, Joachim has made numerous appearances on television and radio.

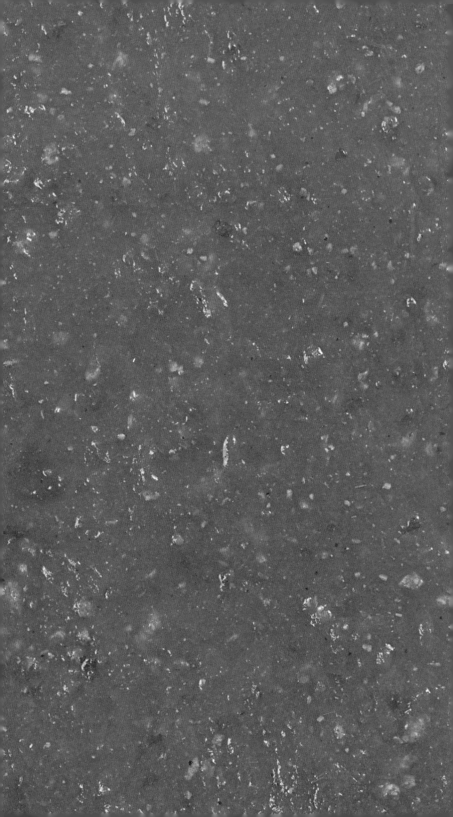